DO YOU HAVE EMPTY NEST SYNDROME?

7 EASY STEPS ON HOW TO OVERCOME YOUR EMOTIONAL DISTRESS

J.T. HAMM

CONTENTS

INTRODUCTION

CAUGHT IN THE WHIRLWIND OF EMOTIONS

Summer is fast approaching, and you sit quietly in your living room, staring at the colorful painting hanging on the wall across the room. Suddenly you find yourself drifting into memory lane, you reminisce on a late spring afternoon, walking from aisle to aisle in the art gallery carefully searching for that one perfect painting that would complement the exquisite yellow and turquoise scatter cushions on your living room couch. You vividly recall the look on your daughter's face, arriving home from school that day. Her pleasant smile lights up the entire room. Dazzled by your artistic taste, she stands in front of the painting admiring the splendor and magnificence of your beautiful new piece of art. Hugging her tightly, you both exchange glances and warm smiles. You gently kiss her forehead and ask, "How was school today?"

"School was great!" she responds. "Remember the assignment I handed in last week?"

"Uh-huh," you replied as you reached out to open the pantry to prepare a peanut butter and jelly sandwich for lunch.

"Well, I got an A+."

"Well done, honey! Told you you would ace it," you responded, handing her the plate and a glass of almond milk.

Suddenly, you are brought back to the confines of your living room by a shattering noise coming from outside. Jumping to your feet, you rush to the door to see what it is. A part of you is excited, maybe your baby is home from school. With eagerness, you swing the door open only to realize it was just your dog that knocked over the flower pot on your front porch. You stand there for a few seconds holding the doorknob with one hand, staring at the broken pieces of the handcrafted piece of pottery scattered all over the floor. Then, reality hits you, you are all alone! Your kids have left the comfort of your nest. Your eldest son got married last year and now lives across town with his beautiful young bride.

Your youngest daughter just moved out to college three months ago. *How on earth is life going to be from here on?*

You spent most of your adult life taking care of the kids. Your routine centered around getting them ready for school, making sure their sports gear is ready for game day; the house is in order, and lunch is ready before they get home from school, helping them with their homework, attending sports practice, and the best part, preparing for their next birthdays. Heck, you might have even quit your entire career just to ensure that the kids had all the support they needed. You had a purpose, something to look forward to every day. *What now?* you wonder. Before you know it, your mind is spiraling out of control with thoughts of how life is going to be without their simple presence lighting up the entire house. You worry about their well-being and find yourself caught in the whirlwind of emotions and you just don't know what to do to feel better. Sounds familiar? It is common for parents, both moms and dads, to grieve when the people they spent their entire lives nurturing finally leave their nest, more so for moms who are the primary caregivers.

Empty nest syndrome is the term used to refer to the loneliness and overwhelming feelings of loss parents experience when children move out of their homes. It is a condition that is often overlooked because it is a norm for children to eventually move out of the home when they hit a certain age. Too often, grieving parents find little or no support during this period, and other major life events, such as retirement and menopause, add to the heap of emotions and sadness leading to anxiety.

WHAT NOW?

In my many years of experience working as a Professional School Counselor, I have helped parents with parental advice and guidance. As the years go by, I have witnessed firsthand how complicated the child-adult relationship can be. The bond between parent and child, more so in moms, goes beyond the physical aspects of the relationship. It is an emotional connection that develops in the early stages of the relationship, stemming from that feeling of intense joy parents experience the day the doctor hands them the pregnancy results or when they sign the final adoption papers and eagerly await to bring home the new member of the family. As a parent, it makes sense for you to want to hold on to that feeling for the rest of your life. Furthermore, as the years go by and you get to know your bundle of joy even better, the bond is sealed tight, and nothing else matters as long as these little souls are protected, healthy, and happy.

While people have given birth and nurtured children for decades, times have changed, and the phenomenon of children leaving home to gain their independence has become a norm. For most parents, however, when the time finally comes to let their children out of their nest, they are caught unaware of the sudden changes that come with an empty nest. A once-busy home filled with laughter and screaming can often feel too quiet giving way to feelings of loneliness and sadness. I decided to write this book as a means of support, to help parents navigate their way through their new life. If you are struggling to deal with feelings of loss and finding purpose after your kids leave the home, I can assure you, you are certainly not alone. I have counseled many families and helped them overcome the distress they encountered as a family unit.

My unique perspective on empty nest syndrome partially comes from my personal experience. As a professional woman that works with children but does not have any of my own, I can admit, when I first learned about the condition, I could not understand why parents grieved when their children left. Throughout my career, I have passionately studied the subject and found that most parents find it hard to transition from mom or dad to being independent again, and it is a valid place to be. I have encountered different parenting situations. Some parents continued to pursue their careers, and other parents put their careers on hold to assume a full-time parenting role. In the end, both families experience the same rollercoaster ride of emotions during the transition. Some claimed having a career allowed them to stay busy and left little or no room to reminisce, while others advised staying busy, finding a new hobby, or volunteering at a local church group helped them find purpose again. All this advice is sound and has worked for many parents and allowed them to gain back control of their lives; however, it is important to keep in mind that we all grieve differently. Navigating your way through the transition will depend on many factors, including your social support system. In writing this book, I hope to provide you with the support and means to help you identify the symptoms of empty nest syndrome, work through your emotions during the transitional period using the seven-step process, reawaken your purpose, heal yourself, and live your best life. I hope that you will find this book insightful whether your nest is currently empty or you are preparing to make the transition.

1

WHAT DOES EMPTY NEST SYNDROME LOOK LIKE?

FIVE SIGNS AND SYMPTOMS OF ENS

When you hear the word grief, what comes to your mind? For most people, grief is associated with the feeling of loss that comes with the death of a loved one. However, death is not the only life event that causes deep feelings of sadness and loss in us. Every significant, life-changing event can lead to grieving, whether it is moving from the house you grew up in into a new place, leaving a lifelong career to start a completely new path, or separating from a loved one. Change of any kind does not come easy because of the emotional attachment we had with the person or thing. It is the same when a parent has to release a child to own their independence. While seeing children grow and gain their freedom is an event worth celebrating and memorializing, it comes with the grief of loss and lifestyle change. It is completely normal to experience extreme emotions and anxiety during this time. You have been their guide, caregiver, chauffeur, cook, teacher, and nurse from the day they came into this world, kicking and screaming. You held them when they took their first steps and rallied next to them, cheering and clapping as they learned to put one foot in front of the other. You watched your children blossom throughout high school, up till their graduation day in college. And yes, there were fights in between and at times you wished you could take a break from parenthood and just be yourself. But the joy that came with knowing that these young souls depended on you for guidance, protection, and support as they navigated their way into the world gave you the strength and the courage to gracefully perform your parental role. Every event has been a milestone worth celebrating. Whether it is the day you watched your child walk down the aisle on their wedding day or the day they graduated from college, even a simple event, such as watching them leave for summer camp, left you teary-eyed.

Empty nest syndrome is a normal grieving process for parents transitioning from parenthood to being single again, which society does not give much attention to.

Every other significant event in our lives has a ritual or celebration ceremony. For instance, we celebrate when a child is born, we celebrate when a child gets married, we celebrate when they graduate, and even when someone passes on, there is a celebration of their life. *Why not commemorate parenthood and the journey you have taken to get here?* It has been quite a journey and not an easy one for most parents. From the sleepless nights, you spent trying to calm your baby down, to changing diapers, to cleaning their wounds and giving hugs and kisses when they hurt themselves, and to teaching them how to walk and talk. You might have given up on some of your dreams along the way to ensure that your children are well taken care of and it was all worthwhile.

While parenting may have been difficult for most parents, having to release a child into the world is even more difficult to do. The pain of losing a role you played for twenty-plus years, the confusion that comes with not knowing what to do in this new phase of your life, and other factors, such as your health and your relationship with your spouse, can all be adding to your frustration. Lifestyle change is never an easy thing to do. For most of your adult life, you probably followed the same routine each day. As humans, we are creatures of habit, and once a habit forms, it takes time to change it and form a new habit. You would agree with me, starting something new becomes daunting as you age.

However, just because something is not easy to do does not mean it cannot be done.

You might be going through the emotions that come with dealing with your child moving out to college or flying to a foreign country for work, or maybe they just got married, and you are wondering how you can handle these emotions you are experiencing. One thing is certain, you are not alone. If you are struggling to cope with grief and you are not sure whether you have empty nest syndrome, the following are the five common signs you might be experiencing during the transition.

Extreme Feelings of Distress

You have said goodbye to your youngest child as they left your nest and moved halfway across the world to study. You are enthralled by your newfound freedom and are ready to take on new adventures. Finally, you can be yourself again and take up that art class you have been meaning to take since your baby was five years old. You can go out, have fun, let loose, and come home at any time; you should enjoy your new found freedom. But then out of the blue, you find yourself sitting in your car by the parking lot crying your eyeballs out. You are lonely and sad, and these overwhelming feelings were not part of your plan.

It can be normal to find yourself caught up in a whirl-wind of unexpected emotions during the transitional period. You were not prepared to be forced out of the role you played for over twenty-plus years. Up until now, you assumed the role of caregiver, and you were responsible for your children's entire well-being. Suddenly, they are old enough to look after themselves, and they can stand on their own. Being an empty nester can trigger a lot of emotions. You might be sad that your children are no longer dependent on you or that you are aging and have to redo your life without as much energy as you had before you had kids. You might be anxious about your relationship with your spouse and your health, or that you have not accom-plished what you had hoped to achieve by now. All these emotions are valid, do not evade them; instead, embrace them while getting involved in activities to counteract these negative feelings.

Losing a Sense of Meaning

It makes absolute sense! Your entire adult life has been centered around building your nest. For years, you worked hard to create a warm, loving home for your children. You have been there from the day they came into this world to the day they first called you *Mama* or *Papa*. You held their hand and helped them take their first steps, and when they fell and bruised their delicate knees, you were there to kiss the wound and provide comfort and reassurance that everything would be alright. You wiped the tears off their faces, hugged them, cheered them, reprimanded them, and celebrated every milestone in their lives from birthdays to choir concerts, to countless sports events. And now, you find yourself losing your sense of identity. *What will life be like from here on?*

It is common to feel like you have lost your sense of meaning. The good news is, with time you will find purpose again and regain the zeal and enthusiasm to take on life, more so, if you focus your attention on a new hobby or take on a new challenge. While it can be tempting to sit and wallow in self-pity, do not lose sight of the beauty that lies ahead—the new beginnings that are unfolding before you, the new experiences in this new phase of your life, and your children's lives.

Frustration Over a Lack of Control

Up until this point, your sole responsibility has been planning your children's lives. With them moving out of the house, you might feel thrown off course and without control over managing every detail of their lives. The lack of control over when your child goes out, who they befriend, what they eat, do, and choose to pursue in life can be frustrating. You might feel excluded from their lives and want to gain back control. It is important to note that how we perceive our lives is not based on what is happening but on how we see ourselves. Your current perception of life may not be the reality of what is happening. Our perceptions are formed from our early childhood experiences, and yet they shape our entire outlook on life. For example, if you suffered a great loss as a child, every other sad experience in your adult life may feel like a tragic loss. When we understand where our motivations come from, we gain control of our reactions. *How does perception relate to an empty nest?* The thing is, how you see this new season in your life determines your behaviors and actions. If you perceive it from a point of lack, all you will see is what you are missing out on. However, if you look through an optimistic lens, you will notice the beautiful new beginnings and vast opportunities that lie ahead.

As you transition, one important thing to avoid is being a helicopter parent. While your heart may be in the right place, trying to guilt trip your way into planning every detail of your child's life even after they leave your nest may lead to resentment. They might even see it as an invasion of their newly found freedom.

Remember the time your child learned to hold a plastic spoon, with slow, zigzag movements they tried to guide their hand toward their mouth. You stood there and watched with adoration, as the spoon landed on their nose instead. You smiled and gently wiped the butternut puree off their tiny nose. That was the beginning of the many valuable lessons you taught them. Trust that they will carry those lessons for the rest of their adult lives. Instead of wanting to hold on to the role you played all these years as commander-in-chief, assume a new role as an adviser. Do not be afraid to let go of your grip; your children will always need your parental advice.

Marriage or Relationship Stress

Is your relationship with your partner or spouse strained? In the course of building your nest, you may have set your needs and your partner's aside. Your entire life has been about the kids and working to provide a comfortable home for them, and now that it is just the two of you in the house, you find yourselves struggling to reconnect. It can take time to find your groove again. Finding activities you both love and are passionate about after spending years indulging in activities that are centered around your children's interests can be difficult at first. You may even find that you have different reactions to your current situation. One of you may be experiencing grief and loss, while the other is quite ecstatic about future adventures. *How can you reconcile your relationship back to its former glory? How do you strengthen the bond and rekindle the flashing spark of desire in your intimate life?* The first step to reconnecting with your partner is to rediscover what brought you together in the first place. You may have met at a concert, for example, because of your love for classical music. But because of the kids, you could not find the time to attend your favorite shows. Now is the time to take on the activities you both love. It could be an old hobby or a completely new passion.

Do not be afraid to have the conversation about how life is drastically changing for both of you now that the kids are out of the house. You would be amazed at how much your passions have changed over the years. Addressing your feelings with honesty paves the way to finding effective ways to heal and support each other that will help you both during the transitional period. It will help you identify if you need to seek professional help or if you need to create a new routine to help you reconnect. For instance, you could plan a date night once a week or take regular walks in the park together if you have not done so in a while. Whatever your idea of fun time may be, schedule time to do activities together.

Anxiety About Your Children's Well-Being

You have witnessed many milestones since the first day you taught your child how to walk or ride a bicycle.

You were there through the highs and lows of the parental rollercoaster ride, from planning birthday parties to rushing into the ER at 2:00 a.m. when they caught a terrible fever and proud moments of helping them pick their prom outfit. Up to this point, you had the most important job in the entire universe, love and instinct guided you every step of the way. You never went to parenting school. No one handed you a PhD and congratulated you on quite an achievement you made in raising your children. Even without going to school for parenting, somehow you graduated summa cum laude in teaching, medicine, psychology, research, and management. Yet here you are under celebrated and about to assume a completely new role in life. You were not prepared for all of this!

It is understandable if you are anxious and frustrated about children's well-being after they leave your nest; however, in the long run, anxiety can harm your relationships and health. It can prevent your ability to function properly and think rationally. You become overly reactive to certain triggers, and often, you cannot control how you react to situations.

In most homes, moms are the primary caregivers. Preparing a home-cooked meal and watching the kids gobble it up brings comfort to them. After they move out of home, it is common to worry about what the kids are eating, whether they are healthy, and making wise life choices. A healthy approach to ensuring that you stay connected with your children is to find a balance in communication and means of participation that works for both of you. I can assure you, keeping track of your child's day-to-day activities, checking their social media accounts, or constantly calling just to remind them not to forget to floss will not be helpful. Being available, however, to listen when they face everyday challenges young adults go through or share the exciting news of their new adventures, goes a long way. As you transition from living in the same house to living separately, you will learn when to initiate communication and when to wait for your child to reach out. Learning to direct your children to the right resources when they need assistance instead of jumping in to save the day and having a hands-on approach in their lives can also prevent disappointment and conflicts. This new season can be a positive experience that leads your children to be independent, responsible adults if you handle it well.

HOW TO OVERCOME EMPTY NEST SYNDROME

Take a moment to think about the following questions: *Who are you outside of being a parent? What would you like to invest your time in that you could not do before?* These questions are a good place to start your healing process. The answers can be overwhelmingly frightening at first, and it is okay to take your time in answering them. There is no need to pressure yourself into solving everything now; after all, slow and steady wins the race!

If you feel a deep void and a loss of purpose after the kids leave home, remember grief is normal with a change of lifestyle. You have played many roles in life, such as sister or brother, daughter or son, friend, colleague, or neighbor, but none can compare to being a parent. Although you will continue to play a parental role in your children's lives, it might not be at the forefront and that could be causing you distress. Empty nest season can be a good time for reflection. Now that you have time on your hands, consider identifying other roles you would like to fill. It could be a great time to explore other interests and hobbies that give you a sense of meaning and purpose. *Did you have a hobby that you gave up on because of time constraints?* Or *perhaps you have always wanted to try something new but you did not have the resources and the time.* In the following chapters, we will explore in detail seven ways that will help you overcome empty nest syndrome and forge your way toward a brighter future.

THE FIRST STEP TO OVERCOMING ENS

MAKING SOCIAL CONNECTIONS

Life is fun when you have people to share ideas with. If you are feeling isolated and alone, it might be the perfect time to consider reconnecting with your friends or finding a new network of like-minded people to spend time with. As our families expand, we somehow tend to lose touch with our old social connections. Family priorities take precedence over social gatherings and our friendships. Now that your nest is empty, you might feel like your social circle is contracting. Gone are the days when you could easily strike up a casual conversation with other parents at soccer practice or parent-teacher meetings. You are probably wondering if anyone else is swimming in similar waters.

As we age, it becomes difficult to maintain social connections. We understand how relationships buffer us from a lot of life's challenges, and we yearn for deep connections with those who share the same interests as us. Studies show that having an active social life can tremendously improve cognitive health, for both men and women, in their golden years and improve the quality of their lives. Now that the children are out of the house and you have plenty of time on your hands, consider rebuilding your social life.

How can you improve your social connections? The following six ways will help you rebuild your friend-ships, create new ones, and help you feel more connected.

Build a Social Network With People Who Share Your Interests

Reconnecting with your old circle of friends could be a good start in rebuilding your social network. You could perhaps reach out to your old college friends, past colleagues, or your neighbor whom you have not had time to catch up with in a while. Chances are, your peers are also going through an empty nest season. This could be the best time to share advice and ideas on how to heal and move forward, as well as explore new passions. If you are starting a new network of friends, consider your interests and passions. *Do you enjoy reading?* Joining a local book club could be a good start in meeting new people who share similar interests with you.

Social clubs are a great place to connect with people while enjoying doing activities you love. You could find a senior center and join a garden club or take up exercise classes if you want to start working on your health goals. Most of these activities do not have a joining fee, and they offer online classes as well. Adult classes can be a good place to meet new people, learn new skills, and expand your mind. Perhaps you love art, consider signing up for an art class, taking up a sewing class, or learning a new language, anything to awaken your creative genius. The learning environment is a great place to meet new people who share your interests.

If you are religious perhaps because of your parental responsibilities you stopped attending church gatherings, now could be the time to revisit your faith-based community. Often, religious sermons are inspirational and can help you cultivate a positive attitude. Meeting like-minded people at least once a week can improve your mood and expand your outlook on life.

Struggling to find a group that shares your interests? Start a knitting club or wine tasting or baking school, and challenge your members to exchange recipes. You could donate those crunchy chocolate-chip cookies and brownies you bake to a local children's home or shelter for the elderly. Giving back can give you a sense of purpose and increase your confidence.

Embrace Change

Most of the shadows of this life are caused by standing in one's own sunshine.

— EMERSON R.W. (N.D.)

The transition from parenthood to being single again can be difficult to embrace. The significant roles we play in life define who we are. Very few roles you have played took up most of your time or were as meaningful at parenting. It is understandable to want to hold onto your identity, especially if you were a full-time parent. The transition can prove difficult at first if you strongly identify with your parental role because parenthood is a fundamental part of your identity. An empty nest can trigger feelings of insecurity, loss of purpose, and a sense of meaning. At times, you might feel like you are fighting yourself throughout the process; however, resisting change can result in stress, frustration, and anxiety.

Resisting the changes you are experiencing is not the most effective way to handle empty nest season. Resistance implies that you feel you cannot experience something new, create beautiful new memories, and rebuild your social life, which prevents you from going out there and living your best life.

To help ease your mind's resistance to change, you will need to do a little introspection. A good place to begin is to outline the positive aspects of your life. You could start by identifying other roles you play, such as wife or husband, daughter or son, sister or brother, friend, neighbor, or in your career. Go over your list and note which roles you could reinvest your time in. For instance, you could start focusing on your relationship with your spouse and find mutual interests. Consider scheduling time to reconnect and rekindle your romantic life.

Cultivate a Positive Attitude

A smile is not just an involuntary response to the pleasures of life which bring us immense joy. We can make a conscious choice to smile at any given time. What are some of the benefits of a smile? Studies show that smiling has a positive impact on your health and general mood. It is a powerful social lubricant that proves how approachable you are. If you struggle to make social connections or to initiate a conversation, the next time you stand in line at the grocery store or work out at the gym, try smiling at a total stranger. It is a great way to strike up a conversation and not only benefits you but also improves the mood of those around you. Science proves that a smile on your face can relieve stress, strengthen your relationships, lower blood pressure, and reduce the risk of cardiovascular disease.

We all want to live longer, healthier lives, and that is a good enough reason to smile often. Research shows that people with a longer life span are people who are happy and maintain a positive attitude. Even with an empty nest, you want to live to see your children walk down the aisle on their wedding day, play with your grandchildren, and still be able to take on physical activities with your spouse.

Are you feeling stressed out? A smile is a great stress reliever. When you smile, you flex your facial muscles; this simple movement sends messages to your brain and initiates the release of happy hormones—endorphins, serotonin, and dopamine. These feel-good neurotransmitters reduce stress, uplift your mood, and help your body to relax.

Express Your Feelings and Emotions

Having a social support system can help you work through your emotions. Perhaps because of raising the kids and juggling work at the same time, your relationship with your spouse took a bit of a strain, but you shoved your problems on the back burner. Now that the children are out of the house, you find your relationship problems slowly creeping back in and adding to your distress. You might be feeling disconnected and struggling to communicate. If your relationship was strained before the transition, an empty nest could further drive you apart.

This could be the perfect time to have the heart-to-heart conversation with your partner that you have avoided for quite some time or consider seeking professional help. Communication is the foundation of any healthy relationship. In order to build strong social connections, you must make an intentional effort to improve your communication with your loved ones. Seeking counseling can provide a safe space to open up about how you feel. Talking can help ease your anxiety and prevent conflicts from flaring. On the other hand, being open to your family and friends can help you articulate how you feel. If a friend asks if you are okay and you are feeling sad, be honest about how you feel, own your emotions, and do not deny them. Talk about what makes you sad, the challenges you are facing, what you are missing, and the things you want to do in this new season of your life. Being honest about how you feel and listening to each other can help your loved ones understand you better; it can strengthen your relationships and help you move forward.

Do Not Use Your Phone as an Escape

Do you use your phone as an excuse to avoid in-person conversations? In this new age of smartphones and the Internet, it is tempting to spend most of our time scrolling our devices in search of answers to the questions that plague us all or trying to find some sort of relief from boredom. However, in the process of spending our precious time staring at the tiny screens of our most treasured gadgets, we lose sight of the beauty that is in front of us; the life we are currently living and the people that yearn for a deep connection with us. While you might feel better by isolating yourself, making human connections can be a great source of motivation and ideas to help you find a new purpose.

Do you rely on your phone to distract you from your present discomfort? While phones are quite helpful in maintaining relationships, by connecting us eye-to-eye with loved ones who are miles away from us, as well as improving our competence, they are changing the way we meet people, interact with each other, and build social bonds. The use of phones while engaging in in-person interaction can lower the quality of time you spend with loved ones. The next time you visit a friend for a lazy afternoon, go shopping with your spouse, or at the dinner table, perhaps consider using an app or internet blocker to prevent distractions and focus on spending quality time and engaging in meaningful conversations. Self-reflection can also help you identify why you prefer spending time on your phone. Ask yourself why you would rather spend time on your phone than spend it conversing with your partner or friends.

Keep in Touch With Friends and Family

Just because the kids are out of the house does not mean you cannot stay in touch with them. Staying in touch with friends and other relatives is also beneficial to your well-being. Studies show that meaningful rela-tionships are the key to living a happy life. Maintaining social connections makes you feel you are a bigger part of your loved ones' lives and gives you a sense of meaning.

Do you feel isolated? Empty nest season can trigger feel-ings of loneliness, isolation, and alienation, which leads to anxiety, depression, and antisocial behavior. Staying connected with your loved ones can help reduce feelings of loneliness and greatly improve your mental health. Fortunately enough, technology has made it easy for us to connect with loved ones even when we are not in the same place. Regular phone calls, text messages, and social media platforms are all excellent forms of communication to help you stay in touch with family and friends. While technology has made it easy for us to communicate, it is important to note that our personal touch is what makes our relationships special. Scheduling time to meet your family and friends in person whenever it is convenient can help you build stronger social bonds. Be spontaneous, go on a weekend getaway, and create new memories. If you live close by, plan regular visits. You could meet over lunch or dinner or grab a cup of coffee and catch up on what has been happening. Remember to send birthday and holiday cards throughout the year, and try not to miss the important events in the lives of the people you love. Every milestone is worth celebrating together, and a personalized gift will mean the world to them.

How can you stay more connected to your loved ones? Video calling applications, such as FaceTime, Skype, and Zoom, are excellent means of communication to maintain long-distance relationships. In some way, it is like talking to your loved ones in the same room, even though you are miles apart. Seeing each other face-to-face gives the conversation a personal touch, allows you to give the people you love your undivided attention, and makes the conversation enjoyable.

THE BENEFITS OF SOCIAL CONNECTIONS TO YOUR HEALTH

We have explored briefly how social connections can improve the quality of your relationships. Now, let us explore in detail the health benefits of being socially connected. Research shows that social interactions can help lower the risk of physical and mental health conditions. Not only does engaging in a conversation with friends and family expand your mind but relationships can also give you a sense of belonging which can improve the quality of your life. We are social creatures, and at the core of our being is our need to be loved and to feel like we belong. If that need is not met, we suffer great pain. We become dysfunctional, and we hurt ourselves and those around us through our behaviors and actions. Social connections are fundamental to the fulfillment of our human needs and overall health.

Research shows that people with strong social connections live longer and experience lower levels of anxiety and depression; they have a better quality of sleep, have higher self-esteem, and are more trusting, cooperative, and empathetic to others. This simple act in turn causes the people around them to respond to them in the same manner. Interacting with other people also lowers stress levels, strengthens your immune system, and increases the rate at which your body recovers from disease. If you are looking for ways to reduce stress, try reaching out to a friend from time to time and recap on the old memories. It will do you good and lower levels of cortisol (the stress hormone) in your body and help improve your mood and alleviate loneliness. Whether it is a simple act of offering help or advice or expressing affection, connecting with your loved ones is beneficial to both you and the receiver. Neurobiological research shows that social interactions help the body to release dopamine (the happy hormone), which reduces sadness and depression. When we are connected to others, feelings of loneliness dissipate. We feel a sense of belonging and a greater purpose. On the other hand, antisocial people tend to have poor physical and psychological health. They tend to develop antisocial behavior and find it difficult to build social skills, such as active listening, and have low emotional intelligence.

As we age, so does every part of our bodies, including the brain. We start to forget tiny details easily. Engaging in social interactions is a great way to promote learning, stimulate the brain, and improve memory function. Studies show that intellectual stimulation, social interaction, and cognitive health are all linked.

HOW TO STRENGTHEN YOUR SOCIAL SKILLS

Do you have difficulty initiating conversations? Learning how to start a conversation and keep it flowing is a skill that can be learned. For some people, striking up a conversation with strangers comes naturally; they always seem to tell the right jokes that light up the room with laughter. However, for some social skills do not come naturally. *Ever cracked a joke among your peers that was met by nothing but awkward silence?* Such weird moments with friends and family are no cause for alarm. The awkwardness soon turns into a joke everyone shares at social gatherings, which strengthens your bond with friends and family. However, if you fumble often, it could lower your self-esteem, hinder you from pursuing a social life, and can lead to social anxiety.

What are social skills? These are verbal and nonverbal forms of communication needed to promote social connection. Improving your social skills is important to your mental health and overall well-being. It makes you likable and approachable. The following seven ways will help you improve your social skills and increase your confidence to reach out and build social connections.

Define What Friendship Means to You

Friends uplift us when we are down. They help us expand our perspective on life and hold us accountable for achieving our goals. As your social circle widens, keep in mind that friends come in all sorts of shapes and sizes. There is the best friend who is there through the highs and lows of life to the friend you meet occasionally and do not forget the friend that calls you at 2:00 a.m. because they are having a meltdown. The bond is stronger with some friends than others. When building a new social network or reaching out to old ones, consider the following questions.

Do they offer you emotional support? Friends offer us support when we are not feeling our best. Interacting and sharing how you feel with supportive friends makes you feel heard and is important to your well-being.

Do they give you sound advice? Having trustworthy friends to share the important details of your life and talk to when making huge, life-changing decisions can help broaden your perspective and help you find different ways to handle situations. Friends who offer helpful advice can help you develop healthy habits and a positive attitude.

Do you feel at home when you are among your friends? Think of that one friend you share common interests with. Whether it is your love for fine wine and delicious cuisine or you both find arts and culture fascinating. Having someone you share interests with can make you feel at home when you are around them.

Be an Active Listener

There are two forms of communication, verbal and nonverbal. To improve your social skills, you have to learn how and when to use each form of communication. The good news is that these are all techniques you can learn and practice over time. Part of strengthening your social skills requires you to practice active listening. *How can you improve your active listening skills?* Maintaining eye contact when interacting with people, whether in person or through video chat, shows that you are present and interested in what the other person is saying. Being an active listener requires paying attention during interactions and staying focused on what is in front of you.

Smiling and nodding your head are also nonverbal forms of communication to let those you are interacting with know that you are listening. In the same manner, looking away during a conversation can be interpreted as you are not interested. These are all nonverbal ways of communication you can use to improve your social skills.

When using verbal communication, in conjunction with nonverbal communication, for instance nodding your head, adding a phrase, such as *I completely understand*, implies that you acknowledge what the other person is saying. If perhaps you did not understand what they meant, ask the person to elaborate once they finish. You want to refrain from interrupting them while they are talking; it can be interpreted as being disrespectful. If you catch yourself having interrupted someone before they finish what they are saying, apologize and ask the person to continue with their point.

Another way you could practice active listening is by paraphrasing what others are saying and asking open-ended questions that require an extensive explanation, such as *Tell me more.* This shows that you are paying attention. If perhaps you have a different opinion from what your friend is saying, the best approach would be to actively listen and allow the person to finish what they are saying without judgment. This gives you time to think of an appropriate response to express your thoughts. Remember, it takes practice to develop a new habit. The next time you call a friend, ask them what they are reading or what television show they are watching, and give them your undivided attention as they respond.

Use Conversation Starters to Keep Communication Flowing

Maintaining social connections can be difficult if you do not know what to say. Conversation starters can help you know how to start and keep a conversation flowing. There are a few questions you could ask the person you are interacting with to keep the conversation engaging and this will help you practice active listening while the other person responds. Finding out what your friend likes or dislikes is a good start. It will also allow you to assess whether you share common interests. Questions, such as *What is your favorite book or what do you enjoy doing in your spare time,* can be an effective way to start a conversation.

Asking about the hobbies and interests of those you are interacting with is another conversation starter that could help keep the conversation flowing. Perhaps your friend loves art, you could ask how they got into art or what inspires their creativity. *Are you an avid foodie?* Ask what recipes your friends are currently trying out. This could be a great way to find a new passion and improve your culinary skills. Once you kickstart a conversation, you would be amazed at how much you have in common with the people you are reconnecting with. Ask about your friend's career, what they enjoy most about their profession or about their family; perhaps, ask how they manage to stay in touch with their adult children who have left home. These are conversation starters you could use to help you build confidence and keep conversations flowing.

Expand Your Social Network

We are creatures of habit, and we function well when we follow a routine. However, doing the same thing over and over can hinder us from pursuing something new. How else can we make new friends and create new memories if we do not pursue something we have not done before? Meeting new people can help you build social connections and strengthen your social skills. So be brave and embrace going to new places, finding new hobbies, and developing new passions.

Are you a philanthropist? Volunteering for a cause you believe in can give you a sense of purpose and help you meet people with whom you share common interests. You could find a local center for the elderly, or if you are passionate about teaching young people, consider volunteering at a youth center. When you find a place that feels like home to you, introduce yourself, ask questions that are relevant to the group, and be an active listener.

Find Healthy Ways to Handle Disappointments

Reaching out to reconnect with people means you are putting yourself out there, and if you have not interacted in a while, you might feel vulnerable and frustrated if things do not pan out as you had hoped. If a friend cancels plans or perhaps you had hoped to connect with a relative but their schedule does not permit, do not feel bad. Disappointments are part of life; how you bounce back from them is what matters. If you struggle with accepting disappointment, consider these options.

Reflect on Your Feelings

Ignoring your feelings can lead to frustration and stress. We live in a world where we have been taught to affirm that we are okay even when we are not. Owning your feelings will help you find healthy ways to move forward from disappointment and help you face the situation objectively. For instance, instead of thinking a friend declined your invitation to lunch because they do not like you, you could change that thought to, *I am disappointed Mandy could not make it today. I was looking forward to spending time with her.* That way, you shift your focus to how you feel instead of assuming what your friend thinks.

Practice Positive Self-Talk

Speak kindly to yourself as if you were speaking to a friend. When we are frustrated, we tend to unleash the inner critic in us. Our thoughts suddenly turn into a stream of negative self-criticism. We blame ourselves and call ourselves all sorts of names. If a friend says to you, "Ooh, I am so dumb!" What would be your response? Chances are you would say, "No you are not! Sarah, you are the most intelligent person I know." Being kind to yourself can help you build the confidence to reach out to people and rebuild your social connections.

3

THE SECOND STEP TO OVERCOMING ENS

SEEKING PROFESSIONAL HELP

When it comes to healing a grieving heart, there is no one size fits all advice for empty nesters. Some parents take longer to adjust to the transition than others. If you have experienced feelings of grief for a longer period, it could be time to consider seeking professional help. Dealing with grief alone can be overwhelming. Speaking to a therapist can help you see the current situation in a different light. Some couples may be going through marital problems, and some parents may be single and going through financial challenges. All these factors can add to the distress, making it hard for parents to cope during the transition, which could lead to mental and physical health conditions. Single parents without a strong support system can feel isolated, alienated, and abandoned. If these feelings are not addressed, it could result in extreme psychological health conditions, such as anxiety and depression. Seeking the help of a mental health professional can help you work through your feelings, provide you with relief, and help you move forward.

Mental health issues are not the only challenges empty nesters face. Around this time, most women would be going through menopause, which affects their mood and leads to sleep problems and slowed metabolism among other health conditions. This can affect their relationship with their spouse. If your relationship was already strained, an empty nest can further drive you apart. In this case, consider seeking help and advice from a marriage or couples counselor to help you work through your feelings, reconnect with your partner, and rekindle the spark in your marriage. Couples therapy can help you find effective ways to support each other. Bringing awareness to the issues that affect your relationship can help you address them and is a great way to develop a deeper sense of satisfaction and appreciation for one another. Talking to a marriage counselor about your concerns can also give you a new perspective on your relationship.

WHY YOU SHOULD SEEK PROFESSIONAL HELP

Do you struggle with extreme feelings of grief, and your emotions are getting in the way of carrying out daily activities? While it is normal to experience grief after the kids leave, there can be an overlap between symptoms of empty nest syndrome and depression. If you are feeling hopeless, experiencing a loss of appetite, having difficulty falling asleep, or feeling inadequate, maybe it is time to seek professional help. Psychotherapy can be an effective way to help you find healing. Although both men and women are prone to experiencing the symptoms of ENS, women are more susceptible. If your symptoms of empty nest syndrome prolong, consider seeking help and advice from a grief counselor to help you work through your emotions. Prescribed medication coupled with psychotherapy can help reduce anxiety and depression. If you feel you have lost your sense of identity, talking to a counselor can help you be more accepting of yourself and allows you to identify your strengths and weaknesses.

Are you finding the things you once enjoyed less pleasurable and nothing fulfills you anymore? A loss of interest in the activities you once enjoyed could be a sign of depression. Without a strong support system, an empty nest can slip you into an extreme state of depression, which could impact your relationships and overall health. Talking about your concerns makes you see them in a different light and allows you to observe life from a different perspective. Through counseling, you are able to identify the issues that hinder you from moving forward and gain a different view of your current situation. Seeking guidance and advice from a counselor can help improve the quality of your life. The following are some of the benefits of seeking professional help to help you gracefully transition.

You Will Have a Support System

Are you having difficulty talking about how you feel with your friends and family? The thing with grief is that it can make us feel like no one understands how we feel. While this may be understandable, keeping everything on the inside only prolongs your suffering. Speaking to a counselor or joining a support group can help you work through your thoughts, feelings, and emotions. A counselor knows how to observe impartially and fairly and will provide you with a safe space to share the critical details of your life without judgment. Having a sense of security and comfort can help you open up and reduce self-reservations making it easy for you to be more open to your family and friends. Sharing how you feel can help those around you find effective ways to support you. For instance, if you decide to go for couples therapy, opening up about how you feel can help your spouse better understand you, and it can help them find ways to support you emotionally.

Joining a support group can also help you find people who share your experience and can relate to how you feel. Some of the benefits of joining a support group include having a safe space to freely express your feelings and validate them. You will also receive ideas, support, and advice from other empty nesters to help you through the healing process. Support groups are a great place to meet new people, learn compassion, expand your network, and alleviate loneliness. Whether it is individual therapy, couples therapy, or family counseling, expressing your feelings and emotions is a good place to start your healing process.

To Help You Maintain Healthy Relationships

Do you feel like you have lost your sense of identity? Earlier, we discussed how the roles we play in life define who we are. When that role is taken from us, we tend to lose a sense of who we are. The transition from being a parent to being single can make you feel like you have lost your sense of identity. Speaking to a counselor can help you face the lifestyle changes that come with an empty nest, which are causing you grief. Counseling promotes individuality and independence and makes you feel better about yourself. In other words, a counselor can help you identify who you are outside of your relationships. When you embrace your individuality, you can build better relationships and define your identity outside the roles you play in life.

Seeking professional help allows you to explore your thoughts, feelings, and concerns. Engaging in a dialogue with your therapist can improve not only your communication but your active listening skills as well. By exploring your thoughts, feelings, and concerns, you can gain a better understanding of yourself, identify your triggers, and find effective ways to manage them. When you are empowered, your perspective on life expands, and when you are healthy and balanced, your relationships reap the benefits. Seeking professional help can help you communicate clearly and honestly in a way that will make your loved ones hear you. Improved communication can elevate your level of interaction.

To Reduce the Risk of Physical Health Conditions

Psychological conditions, such as anxiety and depression, are not the only health issues grief can cause. Stress affects our behaviors and thinking ability. Emotional signs of stress include feelings of low self-esteem, feeling overwhelmed, agitation, and frustration. Behavior signs of stress, on the other hand, include changes in appetite, procrastination and, to some people, the use of drugs and alcohol as a way to cope with stress. Physical symptoms of stress include low energy levels, insomnia, an upset stomach, tense muscles, aches, and body pain. Besides mental health conditions, stress lowers the ability of the immune system to fight disease, making you susceptible to illness.

The side effects of not managing stress over time include physical health issues, such as extreme fatigue, sleep disorders, slowed metabolism, obesity, cardiovascular disease, and diabetes, among other physical ailments. Identifying earlier that you need professional help can reduce the risk of developing these life-threatening illnesses and help you maintain good health. Just because you are grieving does not mean you must put your health last. This is the perfect time to put your health and the rest of your needs first now that you do not have to rush the kids to school.

Seeking professional help also allows you to identify unhealthy behavior patterns before they turn to addictions and with awareness comes responsibility. With the help of a counselor, you can find healthy ways to cope and overcome empty nest syndrome and improve your well-being. A healthy mind equals a healthy body. When you are healthy and strong, you can take on physical activities, such as dancing with your spouse or playing frisbee with your dog, which can help reduce the risk of noncommunicable diseases, such as stroke and heart disease.

To Help You Develop Healthy Coping Mechanisms

When we go through stressful times, the natural response is to find ways of coping strategies to relieve us from the pain and help us move forward. Some of these coping mechanisms are effective in giving us temporary relief; however, these temporary stress relievers can lead to addictive behavior. For instance, unhealthy self-soothing behavior can be in the form of unhealthy eating and binging and the excessive use of alcohol and drugs. If these habits are not dealt with, they tend to turn into addictive behavior over time.

There are two forms of coping strategies: adaptive coping and maladaptive coping mechanisms. Adaptive coping mechanisms are healthier ways in which you learn to adjust to stressful times, such as seeking support and learning relaxation techniques like deep breathing, aromatherapy, or yoga. Other healthier ways to help you cope during adverse times include developing problem-solving strategies to help you manage stress effectively, such as humor, to help you make light of any situation, and physical exercises, such as running, walking, hiking, or dancing, to help clear your mind. Therapy can help you develop healthier ways to adjust to the transition. These healthy coping strategies can help alleviate stress and improve your well-being.

On the other hand, not seeking professional help could result in maladaptive coping mechanisms, such as self-isolation, which can negatively impact your relationships. While withdrawing from friends and family can provide you with temporary relief and give you time to process your emotions, it can drive a wedge between you and your loved ones. Other unhealthy coping mechanisms, such as numbing behavior and the overuse of alcohol and drugs, can lead to long-term health conditions, such as liver failure and lung disease. Without emotional support, stressful times can drive you into compulsive behavior patterns, which can cause you to take risks that could lead you to further distress. Speaking to a therapist can help you re-establish your identity. It encourages your freedom and can boost your self-esteem.

Improves Your Performance at Work

Is empty nest syndrome affecting your work life? It is no doubt that stress can affect all areas of your life, not just your relationship with friends and family but your career as well. Parents with careers are impacted as much as stay-at-home parents. Grief affects everyone, though the way we choose to deal with stressful times differs. Grieving can lead to a loss of interest in carrying out any activity, and it can be more difficult to cope with the pressures of completing work tasks and meeting deadlines. Working through your emotions, through therapy, can help you devise coping strategies, encourage a positive disposition, and help improve your focus and ability to accomplish tasks on time.

The symptoms of grief, such as low energy levels, a lack of motivation, pessimistic thinking, and low self-esteem, can lower your productivity and could affect the entire workflow. These negative effects can cause you to doubt your abilities and could lead to tensions with your colleagues and a bad reputation for you. Negative thoughts can cause you to avoid work activities, such as team briefs or team-building activities, which are meant to build trust in the workplace, help develop employee strengths, and improve morale and communication. Seeking professional help allows you to work through your thoughts and identify behaviors that are hindering your effectiveness at work. Optimized performance at work can help increase your effectiveness and productivity and help you create a work-life balance.

Improves Your Quality of Life

We all want to live healthy and happy lives. That is the ultimate goal. When we are stable and balanced, all other areas of our lives flow with ease. If you struggle with finding balance because of grief, counseling can help you find ways to relax. One of the many benefits of speaking to a counselor is to help you identify coping strategies you can apply in different situations to help improve your well-being. Coping strategies, such as relaxation techniques, can help ease muscle tension, reduce the speed of your thoughts, and improve your brain's ability to function. When the brain is rested, your ability to think rationally is increased, and you can make sound decisions that will improve the quality of your life.

Seeking professional help can provide you with something to look forward to. Being able to identify what you would like to do next in this season can help you develop a blueprint for new passions and interests. Exploring new activities is a good place to start improving the quality of your life. It allows you to identify what makes you feel happy and empowered. A counselor can also help you define your core values. Clearly defining your values can help you make better choices. No matter what you may be experiencing in this season, values can guide you on your path going forward and give you a sense of self. Self-evaluation is an effective way to get to know yourself better. Talk therapy encourages self-evaluation and self-monitoring. The ability to evaluate yourself can lead to a better understanding of your needs and core motivations.

Self-awareness allows you to take progressive action in monitoring your thoughts and behaviors and opens room for positive outcomes.

Seeking professional help promotes the development of new habits. Research at Duke University shows that forty percent of our behaviors each day are accounted for by our habits (Clear, 2014). Habits are key to improving your well-being, and counseling can help you develop healthy habits, such as getting enough sleep, which improves brain functionality. Other habits, such as engaging in physical activities, can help strengthen your heart and reduce the risk of heart disease and other health conditions. Therapy also encourages positive mindset habits, such as journaling, which can greatly improve your memory and help you set and manage your goals.

FIVE SIGNS YOU SHOULD SEEK PROFESSIONAL HELP

Are you unable to articulate how you feel? There are five stages of grief, namely, denial, anger, bargaining, depression, and the acceptance stage. During the first stage, we use denial as a means to relieve ourselves from the pain of loss. Accepting that your parental role is changing can be difficult at first. It can take you time to adjust to your new reality. As your mind reflects on the memories you have shared with your children, you might be having difficulty moving forward.

Do you feel more agitated with friends and family than usual? Pay attention to how you react to everyday stressors; for instance, are things like checking your inbox leaving you enraged? Changes in your mood, behavior, and decision-making process impact your relationships and affect your functionality. If you notice that your reactions have drastically changed, it could be time to consider seeking professional help.

Were you always the first to get out of bed in the morning and prepare breakfast for everyone? Perhaps, because of the kids, your mornings were exciting. The smile on their faces and the smell of coffee and omelets in the kitchen gave you something to look forward to every day. Now you find the atmosphere in the house has changed, and you have nothing to look forward to anymore. Grief can lower your ability to function properly in all areas of your life. Your mood changes and that, in turn, affects your ability to concentrate. A lack of focus can affect your ability to make sound decisions, and poor decisions can add to your distress.

Without a doubt, a lifestyle change can cause stress and anxiety. If you are having difficulty processing your feelings and that is getting in the way of your relationships and career, the following five signs will help you identify if you must seek professional help.

You Have Difficulty Concentrating

You decided to jumpstart your career after the kids left. It is a brand new day; the sun is shining, yet you sit in your office feeling all gloomy. Your to-do list is piling up, and you are having a hard time concentrating or completing any tasks. With no doubt, grief can trigger all kinds of feelings and emotions. An empty nest can trigger a lot of emotions. You might be anxious about your kids' well-being, your future, your relationship with your spouse, and the pile of work on your office desk. All this could be adding to your distress.

Stress is energy-consuming and can leave you with less mental capacity to function effectively. When you are not functioning at your optimum, the quality of your work and relationships become less impressive to those who depend on you. A lack of focus not only affects your productivity at work but also impacts your ability to actively listen. It is understandable to zone out sometimes, but if it is becoming a norm, a lack of concentration can affect your relationships and attitude and lead to a lack of motivation to carry out daily activities. When your ability to concentrate is lowered, you become susceptible to making mistakes and poor decisions. Mistakes in the workplace can cost the organization time and money and result in a bad reputation for you. Poor decisions can cause your family and friends to lose trust in you.

Your Loved Ones Are Concerned About Your Well-Being

We are social creatures, and relationships are the most important aspect of our lives. We feel stable when there is a balance in communication in our relationships. When we experience a change in the relationship, whether we are finding it hard to communicate or there is tension with loved ones, this can be a cause for concern. One thing to remember during the empty nest season is that you are not the only one going through a hard time. You may have other kids as well and your spouse to consider. Your friends and other relatives could also be having difficulty understanding how they can support you. Failing to communicate your needs and concerns clearly can increase tension between you and your loved ones.

If you find that you are constantly fighting with your family. Maybe you feel self-isolation can help you sort out your emotions, and you are avoiding social activities. Not participating in social gatherings could lead your family and friends to further worry about your well-being. It is not every day that we wake up feeling energized; some days we wake up and feel we want to sleep in. However, if you feel you are hopeless and no longer find joy in the activities you once enjoyed, that could be a sign of depression, and it might be time to seek professional help.

You Have Sleep Challenges

Science has proven time and again the benefits of sleep to our health and well-being. To increase your functionality, your brain needs to be sharp. Sleep plays a huge role in memory retention. A good rest aids in the process of learning and remembering, and a lack of refreshing slumber disrupts these cognitive processes. When you are sleep deprived, you can have difficulty recalling details and experiences of the day.

A good rest is like resetting your entire system so you can function at your optimum. Without sleep, your brain has difficulty taking in new information. If you are feeling down and your energy levels are low, try getting a goodnight's rest. Sleep is a great mood and energy booster. When you are asleep, your brain has time to process your emotions. However, when you deprive the brain of its processing time by not getting enough sleep, this results in negative emotional reactions. Not only does sleep improve brain activity but also lowers blood pressure and allows your heart to rest, reducing the risk of cardiovascular disease and stroke.

Depriving yourself of sleep numbs you and reduces your effectiveness. Often, sleep loss tends to worsen the symptoms of depression, which leads to sleeping disorders. It reduces your ability to concentrate and impairs your alertness and reasoning. Besides memory loss, a lack of sleep can affect your sex drive as well. When you are experiencing depleted levels of energy, it is difficult to initiate or participate in any sexual activity with your partner or spouse. You feel less motivated and that is because not getting enough sleep lowers your libido. A lack of affection and not fulfilling your partner's sexual needs could drive a wedge between you and your spouse. To rescue your marriage, it might be time to consider scheduling a counseling appointment.

Nothing Excites You Anymore

Do you remember how you used to enjoy baking chocolate chip cookies? You would sit on the living room couch and take in all that sweet aroma seeping through the oven, or maybe it was the look on your children's faces when you handed them a hot plate of cookies and watched them quickly gobble them all up. Now that the kids have left your nest, you have lost interest in the things that once brought you so much joy. Without a doubt, grief can leave you feeling less motivated to do anything, even the things you love. You can feel less motivated to do the laundry, cook, or even go out. It is understandable, with low energy levels, it can be difficult to carry out physical activities. However, it is important to note that a lack of inspiration to engage in activities that bring you joy, such as spending time with friends and family or indulging in your hobbies, can be a sign of deep emotional issues. It would be best to seek help.

A lack of motivation to carry out daily activities can also lead to a delay in accomplishing your goals. Motivation and goals are closely related. One influences the other. Motivation is defined as the process that drives you into action or that feeling that compels you to carry out a task. If nothing excites you anymore, it can be difficult to find the drive to achieve your goals. Failure to achieve your goals could potentially result in you feeling stuck and could add to your distress. This could be the perfect time to consider speaking to a professional to help you through your grieving process.

You Use Substances to Help You Cope

When we go through a difficult time, our automatic response is to find ways to numb the pain caused by stress. These stress relievers, also known as coping mechanisms, can be long-term or short-term solutions to relieve us from the pain we experience when there is an imbalance. Most people prefer to take the short route to relieve their symptoms of stress by resorting to numbing behavior, such as the use of drugs and alcohol or unhealthy eating. While binging on food can provide temporary comfort and alleviate loneliness, smoking can help you relax, a drink can help numb your thoughts, and the use of sleeping drugs can help you sleep better at night; numbing behavior can turn into an addiction over time.

While self-medicating can give you temporary relief, it can exacerbate your stress symptoms. Whether it is the use of prescribed drugs or illegal ones or you resort to alcohol to help you feel better, temporary stress relievers can result in long-term health conditions, such as mood disorders, lung disease, cancer, stroke, and cardiovascular disease, among other health conditions. If you are struggling to cope without the use of drugs and alcohol, it might be time to consider seeking professional help. With the help of a trained professional in matters of mental health, you can find healthy ways to overcome empty nest syndrome.

4

THE THIRD STEP TO OVERCOMING ENS

SET GOALS FOR THE FUTURE

Do you feel like you have lost meaning in life after the kids left? Perhaps, it is time to look into the future. One of the symptoms of empty nest syndrome is feeling a loss of purpose. When we lose something or someone we love, we tend to look at the past for far too long. Though you have not lost a child, you have to let go of the role you played your entire adult life. Looking into the past can surely provide you with comfort. Reminiscing on the good times you shared with those you love can make you feel happy, but it also keeps you in the past yet there is a future that awaits ahead of you. Setting new goals can provide you with something to work toward. Goals can help you assess what you want in this next phase of your life. Ask yourself, "What would give you a sense of fulfillment right now?"

Why set goals? A goal can be defined as a personal vision for your future. A clear vision can give you a sense of purpose, and once the goal is achieved, that feeling of accomplishment is a great self-esteem booster. We all have dreams and aspirations we would like to achieve in life. Goals are like future projects you would like to accomplish. Giving yourself time to think about what you want for your future gives you a sense of meaning. Goals give you something to focus on each day outside of your present circumstances. Having something you look forward to achieving gives you the motivation to take steps toward its accomplishment.

The most effective goals are specific, measurable, attainable, realistic, and time bound. They allow you to measure your progress. For instance, if you fail to meet a goal, it is easier to identify why you fell short and make amends in the future. Sometimes we are met with temporary failure in life. Goals allow you to assess the small steps you took while working toward their accomplishment. Even when the goal is not met, you will notice that you are not where you began and that

DO YOU HAVE EMPTY NEST SYNDROME? | 65

can motivate you to keep working toward their accomplishment.

What would you like to accomplish in the next six months? Goals can be short term, medium term, or long term. Short-term goals are your immediate goals. Long-term goals, on the other hand, are goals you would like to achieve in the long run. To have an idea of what goals to set, consider your interests. Perhaps because of your love for ceramic art, you would like to start pottery classes in the next two years; this would be your long-term goal. Your short-term goal would be to take up a pottery class and learn how to craft bowls, plates, flower pots, and wedding vases in the next six months. Having a clear picture of where you would like to be in the future gives you something to look forward to; it expands your outlook on life and inspires you to keep moving forward even on days when you feel like you have nothing to live for.

HOW TO SET SMART GOALS

Setting goals gives you control over your life. By writing down your goals, you acknowledge your vision for the future. Being specific about your vision for the future gives you a clear picture of the small steps you need to take to reach the goal. At times, it seems like we are not making progress in achieving our aspirations.

And the reason behind this is that our vision for the future is vague. Specific goals provide clarity and precision and can help you create a new routine. *Not sure where to start?* What are some of your passions? When setting your goals, remember, to achieve them, you must have the inspiration to follow through. Your goals must be something you hold dear, something significant to you that will make you proud once you achieve them. *What does a smart goal look like?* An example of a short-term goal would be saving ten thousand dollars for a two-week vacation with your spouse in the next five months by setting aside two thousand dollars each month. And how is this a smart goal?

The goal is specific. The details are precise, and that is to save ten thousand dollars for a vacation. Being specific about what you want gives you control over your life. Take some time to answer the following question: *what does a life of ease look like to you?* Once you are clear about the goal, it becomes easy to work on the micro-steps to achieve it.

The goal is measurable. You want to be able to track your progress toward the achievement of your goal. To set achievable goals, you must have a breakdown of how you will accomplish them. In our example above, this would be by saving two thousand dollars each month for five months.

DO YOU HAVE EMPTY NEST SYNDROME? | 67

The goal is attainable. Empty nest season can be a great time to invest in the things that bring you joy. Now that the kids are grown and can look after themselves, you might have extra funds to set aside each month for your dream vacation. In our example, the micro goal is to save two thousand dollars each month toward the accomplishment of our goal.

The goal is realistic. *Are you able to achieve the goal within the timeframe you set?* Setting goals you will not be able to accomplish can be discouraging. When you set goals, ensure that they are well within the boundaries of your ability and apply to your lifestyle. For instance, in our example above, is five months a realistic timeframe for you to save ten thousand dollars? And will you be able to save two thousand dollars each month for a vacation?

The goal is time bound. Setting a timeline to achieve your goals gives them a sense of urgency. We all battle with procrastination now and then. Setting a timeline for your goals can help you overcome procrastination and allow you to achieve them within the timeframe you set. Meeting your goals can give you a sense of pride and boost your self-esteem.

FOUR GOALS FOR EMPTY NESTERS

Empty nest grief might have left you feeling uninspired to do anything. However, if you look at it from a different light, it could be the perfect time to focus on other areas of your life. Sure you miss the kids, and the once busy house filled with laughter and shouting now feels quiet and no longer feels the same. One of the many ways to overcome empty nest syndrome is to look at this season with optimistic eyes. Cry if you have to, but look at it as a new chapter is opening up, and ask yourself, *What are you looking forward to as you turn a new page?* The past may be filled with great memories; however, the future holds exciting new adventures that could lead you to doors you have not imagined before.

Holding on to the parental role you played might be comforting and allows you to hold onto your identity, but think of the many roles you can fill that could give you a sense of fulfillment and a purpose. You are a wife or husband, sister or brother, daughter or son, or a friend. You can be a teacher, a business owner, or a philanthropist. Whatever your definition of fulfillment may be, start your goal-setting process from there. Eventually, you will find the things that make your heart sing. Someday, you will look back and realize how much your life has blossomed.

While grief can be causing you distress, there is plenty to look forward to if you can place your focus on what is next. Empty nest season can be a time of transformation and growth. This is the time to redo your life. *What are some of the things you wish you had done earlier on in life?* This could be the perfect time to revisit those aspirations and discover who you are outside of being a parent. *What areas of your life can you start focusing on right now?* Perhaps you would like to start a new career, learn a new skill, or travel the world. *What would make your heart sing?* Setting goals that align with your interests will help you find joy and fulfillment and give you something to look forward to.

Plan a Relaxing Getaway

When did you last take time off from your usual routine to have some fun? Chances are it has been a while and most of the fun activities you participated in were probably centered around what the kids liked. This could be the perfect time to plan something exciting like going camping and getting in touch with nature.

When was the last time you thought about no one else but yourself and put your needs first? An empty nest provides an opportunity to focus on your needs and do the things you love and appreciate most. If you are not sure how to pull off a campsite, consider a glamping resort. Glamping is great for outdoor lovers who enjoy nature gazing but also want to return to a comfortable king size bed to recharge. Glamping resorts have amazing gourmet meals, hot showers, and outdoor hot tubs to help you relax. If you enjoy nature and pampering, a glamping resort could be the perfect getaway spot for you and your partner to reconnect and revive your intimate life. Besides the exciting events and activities you will participate in, being out in nature is fun and can greatly boost your mood.

Taking a short break from your empty nest is not such a bad idea. It can help you clear your head and offers you a chance to experience a new atmosphere. A short break from your usual routine can help you feel relaxed, rested, and rejuvenated. It is a great way to learn something new, such as fishing and white water rafting, and to discover new interests. Going sightseeing and listening to the sounds of nature can stimulate your brain and increase your parasympathetic response, which can help your body relax. If you are feeling less inspired, try to be spontaneous, pack your camping gear, and get ready for some fun time.

Challenge Yourself With Something New

When last did you challenge yourself to try something new? You spent the past twenty-plus years taking care of your family and ensuring everyone's needs were met, and the kids went to the best schools. In the process, you might have put your dreams on the back burner. You had a routine, and as much as following a routine improves your competency, it can keep you in your comfort zone. This new season could be the best time to revisit your old dreams and start living them. Achieving something you have always wanted to accomplish can give you a sense of pride. It is a great self-esteem booster.

Have you always wanted to start a business? Consider enrolling in business school and learning how to start and run a successful business. Perhaps you have always wanted to turn your garage into a workshop for your ceramic art or painting. It is time to get your DIY tools ready and bring your dreams to life. Challenging yourself with something new is a great way to discover new passions, and it allows you to get out of your comfort zone. Pursuing something new can help you develop new skills and discover new experiences. A challenge can be taking on a new career, improving your finances, or focusing on your health and fitness goals. If you have not hit the gym in a while, perhaps consider signing up for a gym membership and challenge your friends to do the same.

Save for Retirement

Have you saved for retirement? Part of looking into the future is securing your finances. Now that the children are out of the house and you no longer have to pay for extracurricular activities, consider funneling some of your funds into your retirement savings. Empty nest season could be a good time to review your finances and budget.

Maybe you were mindful of saving money while raising kids. There is plenty of room, now that you have fewer expenses, to revisit your savings goal. If you do not have retirement savings, you can use this season to create a retirement plan and start preparing for the future. To start saving for retirement, define your savings goal. Having clarity on when you plan to retire and how much the cost of living will be can give you an idea of how to create a retirement plan. Keep in mind that the amount you save will be affected by factors, such as interest rates and inflation. When planning for retirement, time is of the essence. The earlier you start saving, the more time your money has to grow through compound interest.

An effective way to save for your retirement is through a retirement savings account. If you are employed, consider using your employer's plan. Some employers have a 401(k) or 403(b) retirement plan which offers different tax benefits. If you are self-employed or your employer does not offer a retirement plan, you can open an IRA (Individual Retirement Account).

Remember to consult a financial advisor before making any financial decisions.

Keep your health in mind as well when creating a retirement plan. For most retirees, healthcare expenses will become a problem in the future. Funneling funds into your Health Savings Account (HSA) is a long-term goal you should consider saving toward. A Health Savings Account can help you pay for qualified health expenses, such as prescriptions, copayments, and coinsurance.

Build an Emergency Fund

Life can be unpredictable, and one way to ensure that you are protected financially is by creating an emergency fund. Having a soft cushion to land on when the unexpected hits can reduce the stress and anxiety of not being able to pay your bills. An emergency fund can help you meet your obligatory expenses if you were to lose your primary source of income or you are unable to work because of a health condition. To build an emergency fund, take into account all your monthly expenses. Your emergency fund must be able to cover all your living expenses.

How do you build an emergency fund? Creating a budget is the cornerstone of an effective financial plan. A budget will help you track how much money you spend on your obligatory expenses and your discretionary expenses each month.

Create a separate account and automate funds into it each month based on the calculation of your living expenses. Automating payments into your emergency fund account can help you avoid skipping payments. Another important thing to note is to ensure that your emergency fund is easily accessible. Nothing is as frustrating as going through a crisis and not being able to access your funds. *Where can you safely keep your emergency funds?* Liquid cash always comes in handy in the case of an emergency. A savings account is also a good place to save for a rainy day. Most savings accounts have a sweep-in facility, and if you exceed the deposit limit, funds are channeled into fixed deposits and accumulate interest. That way you get to reap the benefits of compound interest in the long run. Keep in mind that extra funds in the bank can be tempting. If you are concerned about spending the money in your savings account, perhaps consider a short-term fixed deposit.

Liquid mutual funds are also a great place to put away money for emergencies. Their minimum investment is low, and they offer a higher return than fixed deposits. Planning for your financial future can help you weather the storm in times of crisis. There are multiple secure investment options you can consider as well, such as

Recurring Deposits, National Savings, or a low-risk Public Provident Fund. It is important to note that investment options come with penalties for premature withdrawals and fixed tenures. Always consult with a financial advisor before making financial decisions.

5

THE FOURTH STEP TO OVERCOMING ENS

TAKE UP A NEW HOBBY

Discovering who you are outside of being a parent can be scary at first for empty nesters. You find yourself with plenty of time on your hands for the first time in years. An empty nest is a great time to consider how you will spend your time now that the kids are out of the house. If you were a full-time parent, you might be struggling to find ways to stay busy during the day and to keep your mind occupied. To overcome empty nest syndrome, you may need to consider changing a few things in your daily routine. As a parent, your daily activities were mostly centered around your children's schedules, and maybe you had limited time to do some of your favorite activities. One of the many ways to deal with grief is to do the things you love that give you joy, fulfillment, and meaning. Consider this as an opportunity to rediscover yourself as you embark on this new adventure. If for now you feel lost and wonder what life will be like without waking up in the morning to prepare breakfast for the kids and driving them to school, it is normal to feel like you are losing your sense of identity. Parenting is what defined you all these years. Rediscovering who you are, your passions, and your interests can be challenging at first, but it is a journey worth embarking on. To improve your well-being and find meaning again, you have to start somewhere.

The beauty of life is that no matter how much we try to search for meaning and answers to the questions we have about our lives from external sources, the solutions are always within us. Self-reflection is an effective way to find the things that ignite your soul. Changing your daily routine requires you to spend time doing a little digging into the things, places, and experiences that you love, and that bring you joy and fulfillment. *What new habits can you develop in this new season?* What are some of the activities you would like to incorporate into your daily routine that align with your values and interests? What places would you like to visit, and what experiences would you like to add to your portfolio of adventures that you have embarked on so far? What would make you feel excited about the future, and what can you do in the present moment that will boost your morale? Asking yourself these questions can help you find meaning, develop new passions, and create a new routine. If you are struggling to change your previous routine, perhaps consider taking up a new hobby.

As you transition, pay attention to the things that bring you joy. These are small windows of opportunity to do something fulfilling, exciting, and meaningful that could set a blueprint for a new purpose. Answering the hard questions, such as *who are you outside of being a parent*, can help you identify your passions, dreams, and aspirations that may be lying dormant that need to be awakened. You had dreams before taking care of the kids that took up most of your time, and those dreams ended up turning into *something I will do someday*. Take some time to reflect; you would be amazed at how long your list of to-do things is. Maybe you have always wanted to take up yoga or a dancing class. This is the time to awaken your passions and pursue something new. You could get certified as a yoga instructor, for instance, and help other empty nesters find healing on their journey. Perhaps your passion is gardening, now is the time to get your hands dirty and plant those colorful succulents and fill your garden with delicately beautiful yellow roses.

Hobbies allow you to get involved in the activities you enjoy, and no matter your personality type, I can assure you, there is an activity you can find that matches your interests whether you are an adrenaline junkie and love to indulge in physical activities, such as hiking, biking, or playing sports. Or you are creative and have a special love for visual art, such as writing or painting. The thought of having something you eagerly await to do in your free time is exciting, but the actual act of doing it can greatly boost your mood and improve your psychological health. In today's world, most people undermine the benefits of hobbies to their health and wellness, more so because in today's society, everyone is chasing the rewards that come with achieving career success. For this reason, only a few people actually make the time to indulge in leisurely activities. There are many reasons why people take up hobbies. For some, it is for relaxation and to improve mental wellness, and for others it is for fun and to challenge their minds to improve their critical problem-solving skills. Hobbies are not only beneficial to your health but also your professional life. Stimulating your brain inspires creativity and can improve your competency at work. Doing the things you love can help reduce anxiety and alleviate stress and loneliness. If you are worried about how you will spend your days now that the kids are out of the house, a hobby can be a great source of inspiration for your next adventure. Remember, your personality plays a role in helping you pick activities that align with your values. The following hobbies can help you discover new interests and passions and to overcome empty nest syndrome.

HOBBIES FOR EMPTY NESTERS

Start Journaling

Journaling is known to improve physical and psychological health. The process of journaling goes beyond just putting your thoughts down on paper; it is beneficial to your well-being. If you have not had time to journal in a while, it is time to get that notebook out of your drawer or visit the bookstore to purchase a new one. The following points will help you make journaling a part of your daily routine.

Identify a Method That Works for You

If you cannot journal every day, do not put pressure on yourself. Start by doing it once a week. If perhaps a notebook and a pen do not work for you, consider downloading an online notebook on your tablet, smartphone, or laptop. Online notebooks have a voice recording option. You can use a recording device to speak and record your thoughts.

Let Go of Judgment

Writing your thoughts and feelings in a notebook can help you sort them out and identify your needs and how you can meet them. Remember you are writing for yourself, and the goal is to find healthy ways to work through your emotions. As you journal your thoughts, practice self-compassion and try not to let your inner-critic takeover.

Do a Self-Assessment Often

Journaling is an effective way to track your progress. It allows you to assess how your thoughts are changing, what is working in your new routine, and where you need to make adjustments. Writing down your thoughts and feelings can give you a new perspective on the matters that cause you stress. To top it off, you gain a better understanding of yourself and learn how to cope during adverse times.

Reinforce Your Learning Skills

Empty nest season could be a great time to learn new skills and improve on old ones. If you are feeling stuck, active learning can help to expand your mind and open you up to a new perspective on life. There are a few ways you can explore to promote active learning based on your passions and interests. Perhaps you love music, so why not learn how to play a musical instrument? You could learn how to play the guitar, piano, saxophone, or violin. Learning to play a musical instrument can help you improve your organizational skills and teach you breathing techniques and rhythms that are beneficial for relaxation. *Are you an avid foodie?* You could take up cooking lessons. This could be an opportunity to try out new recipes and different techniques to create a restaurant experience in your kitchen. *Do your baking skills need polishing?* Now that you have time on your hands, consider putting your baking tins to use and start exploring new dessert ideas. Baking can help you relax, and it stimulates your creativity. By exploring different flavors and decorations, you awaken your creative side.

Enhancing your learning skills is a great way to exercise your mind. Perhaps you have always wanted to learn a new language. Consider enrolling in a language class. Learning a new language can expand your outlook on life, help you connect with more people, and boost your confidence. When you master your skill, you could also start classes and teach others how to bake, play a musical instrument, or learn a second language. Teaching others your skill is a great way to validate your knowledge and learning experience.

Sharing knowledge helps others to learn, and at the same time, you feel accomplished.

Take Up Physical Activities

Physical exercise is the best thing you can do for your health at any age. Working out promotes physical vitality and can improve your mood. If you have not worked out in a while, you can participate in a plethora of activities, including swimming, jogging, walking, dancing, chair yoga, biking, or hiking. As you put your muscles to work, you enable your body to burn calories, ensuring your blood vessels stay healthy. You also reduce the risk of heart disease. Not only does exercise improve blood flow but also it allows your body to release fat which it uses for energy in your muscle cells during a workout. Working out is an effective natural weight loss remedy when coupled with a healthy diet.

As we age, our bodies change as well. Our energy levels become lower, and we experience muscle loss, sleep problems, and low sex drive among other challenges. Working out helps the body to release hormones that increase the muscle's ability to absorb amino acids, which helps to strengthen the muscles and repair body tissue. Regular exercise can boost your energy levels, and add years to your life span. Some of the health benefits of physical activity include improving cognitive function, which helps you fall asleep faster and deepens your sleep.

Want to improve your sex life? Working out is an effective way to boost your energy levels and increase your confidence in the way you look and feel about yourself and can improve your intimate life. Finding an activity you and your partner enjoy can be a great way to reconnect and have someone to hold you accountable.

Find Outdoor Activities You Love

Going out into the outdoors, especially in summer, can be quite refreshing. It is a great way to unwind and take in the fresh air. Outdoor activities promote social interaction and encourage exercise, which is beneficial to your health.

Do you love growing your own food or perhaps growing plants? Gardening is a great way to spend your afternoons now that you have the time. It promotes physical movement and increases your energy levels. Believe it or not, gardening can help you feel a greater sense of purpose and reduce feelings of isolation. Whether it is the smell of wet soil or the feeling of digging through the soil to plant a seed or picking ripe fruits and vegetables, gardening can be a relaxing exercise.

When was the last time you packed a picnic basket with all your favorite goodies and spent the afternoon basking in the sun at the park? A picnic is a great way to spend your day outdoors soaking yourself in vitamin D, which is great for your skin. Maybe you have a passion for visual arts, consider taking your camera along with you to your next picnic and capture the beautiful memories you will experience with your loved ones. Outdoor activities are an excellent way to spend time doing the things you love. Whether it is hiking, golfing, fishing, paddling, cycling, or playing tennis, being out in the open can encourage social interaction and improve your focus and learning.

Find a Cause You Believe In

Think about your core values for a second—*what do you stand for?* When we identify what we value the most in life, we can find meaning and purpose. Finding ways to make the world a better place gives us a greater sense of purpose. Empty nest season is a great time to think about what you stand for and where you can make a difference in your community. Whether it is fighting for human rights, protecting the environment, or finding ways to alleviate poverty, identify the gaps in your community that you can fill. Finding meaning and purpose can be in the form of doing acts of good and supporting the vulnerable in your community. When we do good, we feel uplifted, and when we uplift others, we create a world of good where there is little discrimination.

Once you have identified a cause, research its history and foundation and gain a better understanding of what you are fighting for. Note the changes that have been made in the past and whether they align with your values. When you have a better understanding of the group or organization you want to support, it will be easier to reach out to the organizers or advocates of the movement to learn more. Educating yourself on the history of the organization can help you build awareness in your community and on social media about the movement. Social media platforms are a great place to educate others, start petitions and fundraisers, and organize community events to help spread awareness. Standing for a good cause can help you find meaning, improve your social skills, and boost your self-esteem.

Start a Blog and Enhance Your Writing Skills

The internet has made it easy for us to share ideas and educate and build awareness of the things we value most. We spoke about enhancing your learning skills to promote learning. Taking up writing is another great way to spend your time. Writing allows you to awaken your creative genius and enhance your research skills. *Do you have a subject you are passionate about?* If not, you could write about empty nest season and share your ideas, experiences, and challenges.

You could start a blog dedicated to parenthood. A blog can help you build a community that shares a common interest with you. It allows you to connect with parents, share your experiences, and alleviate loneliness. On top of that, you can turn a blog into a stream of income by posting affiliate links to the products and services that have helped you handle empty nest season. For instance, it could be a book you purchased on Amazon. When you share your affiliate link, you can earn a commission when your friends purchase products and services using your referral link.

Blogging can be a form of journaling. By sharing your thoughts, you open up about your feelings and that alone can greatly improve your mood. Writing about your empty nest journey can help you track your progress and allows you to observe how you are advancing in your healing process. A blog also allows you to connect with other parents, who are in a similar situation; it can also be an opportunity for you to help those who are struggling. Focusing on helping others can take your mind off your problems, and it gives you a sense of fulfillment.

Finding activities that can get you out and about will help you connect with other people and expand your mind and learning experience. Choosing hobbies that you enjoy and have an interest in is important to make sure you follow through. Take your personality into consideration when choosing an activity to participate in. It is fun to do something you have a strong interest in and find pleasure in.

6

THE FIFTH STEP TO OVERCOMING ENS

RECONNECT WITH YOUR PARTNER

re you struggling to reconnect with your partner? Great relationships do not happen overnight. It takes years of practice to learn how to build and maintain a successful marriage. It is common however, after being married for a long time to take your partner for granted and put the things that helped to sustain the relationship aside. As parents, your focus might have been on raising the kids and you might have neglected your relationship needs. Now is probably the first time you find yourselves alone in the house in a long time, and it might be difficult to reconnect. Rekindling the spark in your marriage might prove difficult at first especially if you share different views on your current situation, but it is possible. It requires patience and effort from you and your spouse. An empty nest is a perfect opportunity to start focusing on your relationship, go on dates, and interact more. In order to support each other you must be intentional in your attempt to improve communication with your partner. Studies show that 63% of couples become closer to their partners after their children leave home.

The first step to reconnecting with your spouse is to identify the things that brought you together. Talking about good memories can reignite positive feelings and allow you to connect over shared experiences. *When was the last time you talked about how you met?* Share the details of your love story over a glass of wine and express how you felt. Remind yourselves of the things that you love most about each other and what brought you together. These tiny moments you spend talking about the good times can remind you of what makes your love unique. Finding ways to reconnect can help strengthen your bond and help you develop a deep appreciation and affection for each other.

HOW TO RESCUE YOUR MARRIAGE FROM ENS

Now that the kids have left home, what next? How can you revitalize your relationship? Some couples live together for years believing their relationship is vibrant. When the last child finally moves out, they are hit by the reality that things have not been working for years, and they were both just cohabitating for the children's sake. They find themselves in an empty nest and realize that the warmth they felt in their home was because of the kids. Most of the activities they indulged in were centered around their children, and now that the kids have left home, they have nothing in common, and they have difficulty reconnecting. It is normal that parents may develop different interests during the child-rearing years. As we mature and get exposed to new people and new environments, our interests change as well. The key is awareness. When you understand and accept that you both have changed, you eliminate the resistance of holding on to the image of how things were before and embrace the relationship you have now. Communicating your concerns about your relationship and the future without fear of judgment can also help you better understand each other.

Research shows that from the early nineties to date, the rate of divorce has drastically increased with couples between the ages of 50 to 60. Among other factors that lead to an increase in separations, such as finances, one notable factor is that couples spend their child-rearing years neglecting their relationship and focusing more on their children's needs. They later find that they have nothing in common once the children leave. *What can you do to restore your relationship and eliminate the frustration of being disconnected?* There are plenty of ways to bring back the spark in your marriage if you are both willing to do the work, starting with taking care of yourself. When you are going through a stressful time, your energy levels might be low. You might be having difficulty sleeping or staying focused and have little motivation to work on your relationship. Keep in mind that your body and soul need time to recover, so get some rest and be ready to explore the following ways you can implement in your relationship to help you reconnect with your spouse.

Allow Yourself to Be Vulnerable

For most people, expressing their vulnerability to their partners is rarely a comfortable thing to do. However, it is a valuable component in building a healthy relationship. To maintain healthy communication, being open, vulnerable, and understanding with your partner are important elements of nurturing your relationship. *When you think of vulnerability, what comes to your mind?* For most people, it is feelings of fear, shame, and uncertainty. To many, vulnerability is associated with rejection, which can lead to self-reservation and avoiding being seen as weak. Although it can be uncomfortable, being vulnerable can bring about authenticity, genuine love, acceptance, and joy into your relationship.

Vulnerability allows you to embrace your authentic self without the need to please anyone else. By embracing who you are and allowing your partner to witness your authenticity, you can build a healthier relationship where you are accepted, and it is safe to talk about your concerns without the fear of rejection. Allowing yourself to be vulnerable can help you develop empathy. When you can express yourself and share your feelings without holding back, you encourage your partner to do the same. This allows you to better understand one another and create an atmosphere where you can both forgive each other and willingly express your love. Often, grief can leave you feeling like you are misunderstood. Being vulnerable to your partner allows you to work through your emotions and not evade them, and working through your emotions promotes better emotional and mental health.

Create a New Routine

Now that you have time on your hands, why not start planning date nights and other fun activities you both enjoy? You could take turns planning where you would like to go on your next date. Doing activities together can help reinforce your partnership and team spirit. It is a great way to remind yourselves that you can have fun outside of being parents. Couples with common interests tend to have a stronger bond. However, you still have an advantage if you do things alone or with other people. Your differences can lead to great conversation starters. For example, if your partner enjoys watching a soccer game on Saturdays and you do not enjoy the game, you could spend the afternoon catching up with friends over lunch.

Commit to doing something together every week. Do you enjoy bowling? Go to a bowling club once a week. If you are both creative, you could join a paint and wine course and express your creativity while bonding. If you prefer spending time indoors, why not spend Sunday afternoons playing board games? By engaging in activities and playing games that inspire your creativity, you both expand your minds and have fun together while building a healthy relationship.

If you are religious, attend church services together. Sermons can help strengthen your faith and help you develop compassion. Church gatherings are a great place to meet couples you could invite over for Sunday lunch. If you are both philanthropists, volunteering at church and organizing fundraisers can also give you something to look forward to and help you create a new routine.

Be Curious

Remember when you first met, how you would spend hours talking and laughing and never get tired of each other? You wondered if your partner liked the movie you just watched or what they like to eat, what their favorite color is, and what restaurant they preferred. You would listen as they narrate their childhood experiences, interests, and aspirations. *Remember how you felt about planning the future together?* How would you feel if you could experience that feeling all over again? One of the many factors that lead to disconnection in relationships is taking out the element of curiosity. At the beginning of a relationship, we ask our partners a lot of questions. We are eager to get to know each other. As the relationship grows, we become familiar with them, and our curiosity slowly fades away. The longer you stay with your partner, the fewer questions you ask. However, the feelings of nervousness, excitement, and curiosity you felt in the beginning stages of your relationship were the building blocks of the relationship you have today. It was your curiosity that propelled you toward getting to know each other better.

As we grow, a lot changes in terms of our interests, passions, goals, and our outlook on life. *How do you bring back curiosity in your relationship?* To learn something new about your partner, ask them open-ended questions, such as *how do you feel now that we have time for ourselves*, and listen to their response to understand and not just to respond. Actively listen to your partner's response and stay engaged in the conversation to show them you are interested in what they are saying. To maintain the spark in your marriage, do not let your curiosity about your partner fade just because you have been together for a long time. There is always room to learn something new. Maintaining curiosity increases your appreciation for your partner and prevents you from taking them for granted. It deepens your affection and love for each other. Instead of being two humans who are coexisting, curiosity can help you improve your communication and strengthen your bond.

Know Your Spouse's Love Language

People do not communicate the same in relationships. It is important to learn your partner's love language to find out how you can make them feel better during this transition. You may have been expressing your love and affection to your partner, but have you been communicating it in a way that they understand and receive it? Knowing your partner's love language can help you understand how to better communicate with them.

Gary Chapman came up with the concept of the *"five love languages,"* gathered from his years of experience in marriage counseling. In his book, *The 5 Love Languages:*

The Secret to Love that Lasts (Chapman, G.D, 2017), he describes the five styles of communicating love and care and how to use them. Let us explore the *"five love languages"* in detail, as described by Gary Chapman, and how you can use them to effectively communicate with your partner and revitalize your relationship.

Words of Affirmation

People whose love language is words of affirmation value expressing love, affection, and appreciation through words. Does your spouse enjoy praise, kind words, or surprise cute text messages? Bring joy into their day by sending a text message and complimenting them on how good they look.

Quality Time

How does your partner feel when you take time off from work to spend the day with them? Do they feel loved and appreciated when you are present? People who value quality time feel adored when you desire to spend time with them. They not only want to be in your presence but also value active listening, eye contact, and your undivided attention when interacting.

Acts of Service

What is your partner's reaction when you go out of your way to help them and make their life easier? How often do you help around the house by doing the dishes, laundry, vacuuming, or running errands? If your spouse's love language is an act of service, they believe that actions speak louder than words. Making them a cup of coffee in the morning or bringing them a bowl of vegetable soup when they are down with a cold will make them feel appreciated.

Gifts

A gift from someone you love, no matter the size, can make you feel loved. Buying your partner something meaningful to them shows how much you value and care for them. It is not the size of the gift that matters most to people who enjoy physical gifts. It is the effort and thoughtfulness of the giver and the emotional benefits that come with receiving a special gift that they value most.

Physical Touch

Besides sex, people with this love language, value spending time cuddling, touching, holding hands, or getting a relaxing massage. If your partner enjoys phys-ical intimacy, make time to cuddle on a lazy Sunday afternoon or in the evenings while watching your favorite television show. Kiss them every chance you get, and hold their hand when you go out or take a walk in the park. It is these tiny gestures that will make them feel appreciated and help you rebuild your relationship.

Be Adventurous

In the early stages of your relationship, you went on dates. You would explore new places and try out exciting new activities together. As time went by, you fell into a routine. While it is normal to fall into a routine when you do the same things daily, it keeps you in your comfort zone and prevents you from exploring new adventures. Bringing that element of adventure into your relationship again can make things exciting and evoke feelings of happiness. To bring back the sense of adventure in your relationship, reintroduce spontaneity to your routine. You might not have the same interests, but having a common goal can help you work together to achieve it. For instance, if you both decide to go mountain climbing, it means you both share the same goal, which is to reach the top of the mountain, even when you know it is not going to be easy. Your desire to get to the top will ensure that you help each other along the way which teaches you how to work together as a team.

Do something new together. You could plan a date and go to a restaurant that serves food you have never

102 | J.T. HAMM

tasted before. Or plan a zip-lining date and enjoy spending time outdoors. Spending time doing something new can reignite your love and passion for each other. When you pick activities to do together, remember it is the experiences that matter the most. When you go on a weekend getaway, it is the happy moments, such as the couples spa treatment, that you will remember after and not the negatives, such as the flight delay at the airport. Going on adventures together allows you to create new memories and reminds you of how happy you are together.

Build Love Maps

In the beginning stages of a relationship, we are curious about the other person. We pay attention to the tiny details of their personality, from the things they like to their reactions to certain situations. As the relationship progresses, we ask questions, such as what they enjoy doing in their spare time or how they like their coffee. All these tiny details expand our curiosity about the other person. By asking these questions and paying attention to your partner's personality traits, you are building a love map.

In John Mordechai Gottman's (2018) book, *The Seven Principles for Making Marriage Work*, he explains the seven principles and their connection to each level of the *"sound relationship house."* According to Dr.

Gottman, the walls that hold *"the sound relationship house"* are *"commitment and trust,"* which are the building blocks of a healthy relationship. The first level of the *"sound relationship house"* is knowing each other's worlds by building love maps. Studies show that emotionally intelligent couples know their partner's world and keep updating the details of their spouse's life as they evolve. They are familiar with each other's dreams, aspirations, goals, and concerns as well as remember every important event in their partner's life.

From a deep knowledge of each other stems love and affection and the ability to gracefully navigate your way through difficult times. To help you build a love map, take some time to answer the following five questions;

- *What was your partner wearing on your first date?*
- *What is your partner's favorite hobby?*
- *What does your partner fear the most?*
- *What is the one thing your partner dreams of accomplishing?*
- *What are some of the concerns your partner has right now?*

By answering these questions, you can gain a better understanding of each other's lives. Remember, getting to know your spouse is a lifetime process that requires constant updating of your love map. A better understanding of each other can help you build a stronger connection.

Create Shared Meaning

Besides the fun times you have with your partner and the dinner parties you attend, a relationship has a spiritual side that involves creating an inner life together. *What culture or rituals have you adopted over the years that enrich your relationship?* Having a deep sense of appreciation for the roles each of you plays and the common goals you share in your marriage can help you better understand the essence of your union.

How do you create shared meaning? Creating traditions and rituals for your relationship can be a good start. Talk about the traditions from your childhood, and share what they mean to you. Ask each other questions about what you hated the most about the ritual and what you loved. Share how the traditions and rituals from your childhood impacted you and how you feel about them now. From these experiences, you can create shared meaning together. For example, you could create a morning routine that involves waking each other up first thing in the morning, having breakfast together, working out, or taking a morning walk together. Whatever ritual you value most, do it together. Creating rituals and traditions for your relationship can help you create a new routine. It can also help you build a stronger emotional connection.

Revive the Dream

What dreams did you have before you met your partner? Growing up, you had your dreams and aspirations; however, when you met your partner, a new set of dreams emerged as your individual aspirations mingled together to become one dream. The benefit of having a shared dream in marriage is the effect that comes with combined effort. You can achieve greater things together than with individual effort. A shared dream can bring a deep sense of connection and reawaken your passion. When you work toward a common goal, it shows that you are both willing to support each other along the way and that can strengthen your commitment. Working together to achieve a shared dream reinforces team spirit. Whether it is working toward creating financial stability to help you live comfortably after retirement or you would like to move from the city and purchase land in the countryside, a shared dream can bring you closer to each other, and its accomplishment can bring you both joy and fulfillment. The combination of your efforts, experiences, talents, and passions can bring about a unique synergy that can help you overcome the challenges of married life. *How do you revive the dream?* Take some time to answer the following questions:

- *What brought the two of you together?*
- *What goals can you and your partner pursue together?*
- *Where do you want to be in the next five years?*
- *What would you like to accomplish in the next 10 to twenty years?*
- *How do you want to be remembered?*

A shared dream can bring you together to create beautiful, new memories. While an empty nest can feel lonely, it can be an opportunity to rebuild your relationship and pursue something new. When you accomplish your dream, look forward to a new pursuit and continue imagining your future together. Never cease to work as a team toward the achievement of a new dream. Finding ways to reconnect with your partner and nurturing your relationship can help you heal and move forward to a brighter future.

7

THE SIXTH STEP TO
OVERCOMING ENS

PRACTICE SELF-CARE

Self-care is an integral part of any healing process. Over the years, you probably put your needs on the back burner as you performed your parental obligations and ensured that your home was a warm and safe space for your children to grow up. I can assure you, you are not alone. Healing comes in many forms, but it starts with making a conscious decision to do certain things differently. Your soul may be yearning for soothing and rest right now. Grief can take a toll on your mental and physical health. You might not even have the energy to make changes right away; however, you must stay mindful of your health and well-being. An empty nest is the perfect opportunity to create a new self-care routine and refocus your attention on yourself. You can finally relax!

For the longest time, your life was centered around ensuring your family's needs are met. Now is the time to put your needs first—no more rushing to drop the kids off at school or attending parent-teacher meetings and soccer practice. Although you must admit, you do miss game day, right? The transition can be hard at first, but learning to relax begins with tiny moments, such as planning time to watch your favorite television show or taking an evening bubble bath with shower bombs to help you relax. Curl up with a good book and enjoy reading while sipping on your favorite drink.

If you are feeling exhausted, it is because stress increases cortisol (the stress hormone) in your body, which affects your sleep and energy levels. Take some time to rest and rejuvenate. If you struggle to relax, consider finding other options to help you stay in the moment. Meditation, for instance, and breathing exercises can help calm your mind and increase your energy levels.

WHY IS SELF-CARE IMPORTANT?

What comes to your mind when you think of self-care? Do you think of putting your needs ahead of everyone else's? Or perhaps you think of doing a yoga or meditation session or working out at the gym. Either way, you are right. Self-care comes in many forms, but in general, it is defined as making a conscious effort to take care of the six dimensions of your wellness: physical, emotional, spiritual, social, mental, and vocational well-being. Taking care of yourself means putting your wellness needs first. Practicing self-care requires creating a routine and practices that will help improve your overall health. *Why should you prioritize self-care?* As a parent, you probably gave your entire being to loving and caring for your family and ensuring that they live comfortably. The question is, who takes care of you and ensures that your needs are met? Prioritizing your needs can help you shift your focus from your current situation and help you realize that you still have a life to live even with an empty nest.

Following an effective self-care routine can help improve your immune system and brain functionality, reduce stress and anxiety, and promote better emotional health. Self-care practices, such as working out, finding a purpose in life, and better sleep, can greatly improve the quality of your life and increase your lifespan. To some people, putting your needs first feels like selfishness especially if they have put other people's needs ahead of theirs for a long time. However, taking care of yourself, in a way, gives you the ability to help others. Putting your well-being first allows you to fill your cup first before you pour into others.

THE SIX TYPES OF SELF-CARE

Self-care is not only about finding ways to help you relax, it allows you to create a balance between the six dimensions of your wellness: physical, emotional, mental, spiritual, vocational, and social well-being. At some point in life, you might find that you need to focus more attention on one specific area of your well-being to create a balance and find harmony. Below are the six types of self-care and the practices that you can incorporate into your daily routine to help improve your well-being, and live a happier and balanced life.

Physical Self-Care

To function effectively, you need to take care of your physical health because there is a strong connection between your mind and body. Taking care of your physical body not only helps you to feel energized but also improves cognitive function as well. Physical self-care includes having a balanced diet, working out, getting enough sleep, taking care of your body's needs, and staying hydrated. Meeting your physical needs also means getting medical attention and seeking health care advice whenever necessary.

Getting enough sleep is also part of physical self-care. Getting enough rest allows you to reset your entire body and improves brain functionality. It can help you focus and allows you to function at your optimum. A healthy diet and staying hydrated gives your body all the nutrients it needs to improve its performance. Healthy eating requires you to be mindful of what you eat and how you prepare your food. Some of the health benefits of a healthy diet include managing your weight, reducing the risk of heart disease, strengthening your bones, and improving your mental health. Taking up physical activities is a great mood booster. A simple 30-minute walk each day can leave you feeling and looking great. You can try other physical activities such as yoga and hiking, to help you maintain better physical health. Take a few minutes to answer the following questions:

- *How many hours of sleep are you getting each day?*
- *How often do you exercise?*
- *Are you feeding your body the nutrients it needs to stay healthy?*
- *What can you do to improve your overall health?*

Taking care of your physical needs allows you to focus on other self-care practices and helps you stick to your routine.

Emotional Self-Care

Taking care of your emotional well-being is an essential part of your life. Emotional self-care includes taking time to reflect on your feelings and emotions. Carrying out a self-assessment now and then can help you identify the areas of your life that cause you to stress and can help you develop strategies to manage them. Developing healthy habits to help you cope during tough times, such as managing stress, is a form of emotional self-care. When you are aware of your emotional triggers, you can find effective ways to manage the situation when it arises. Taking care of your emotional needs includes seeking help and advice from a counselor or a trusted friend when you feel overwhelmed, journaling your thoughts, posting uplifting notes in your house, practicing gratitude and mindfulness, and maintaining social connections.

To help you improve your emotional self-care routine, ask yourself the following questions:

- *What are some of the healthy ways you use to process your emotions?*
- *What activities can you incorporate into your daily routine that can make you feel better about yourself?*

Cultivating emotional wellness can help you find happiness and feel balanced. When you are emotionally balanced, you see life through optimistic eyes and bring a positive attitude into each day.

Spiritual Self-Care

Making a deliberate effort to take care of yourself and prioritizing your well-being allows you to show up each day despite the challenges you face. Spiritual self-care is another important dimension of wellness. Just like exercise and a healthy diet are essential to nurturing your body, spiritual self-care is essential in helping you stay grounded. *How do you nurture your spiritual wellness?* Taking care of your spirit involves doing practices that help you develop a deeper sense of meaning and connectedness to the entire universe. Creating a ritual or spiritual practice can help you connect with your higher self. We live in a world where fear has a grip on us. We are afraid of what the future may hold, or whether or not we are in the right career, we are afraid to take a leap of faith and do the things that make our hearts sing. Practicing spiritual self-care can help you get out of your own way so you can live a happy and fulfilling life.

By taking care of your spiritual needs, you deeply connect with your higher self. Your higher self is who you are at the core of your being, which is driven by your desires, and what you value most. Practicing spiritual self-care not only helps you to find peace and calm but can also help you find purpose and meaning in life, increase your connection to your intuition, and help deepen your connection to others. *Not sure where to start?* The following spiritual practices can help you create a spiritual routine and promote body and mind connection.

Meditation

Meditation is a great way to help you connect with your higher self. It is an effective practice to help improve your focus and reduce stress. Practicing meditation increases self-awareness. When you dive deep inside and get to know yourself, you become comfortable expressing your individuality and become more accepting. Realizing that you are a big part of the universe helps you develop a deep sense of connectedness and belonging.

For some people, it may be hard to sit in silence for a few minutes to help calm their minds. If you think you cannot meditate, remember, no one is better at meditating than the other. The goal is to make a conscious effort in taking care of your spiritual needs and well-being. You are doing it for yourself and no one else. If you struggle to keep your mind calm, try listening to a guided meditation app, such as headspace or calm. It will help you focus your mind and elevate your positivity. Add some essential oils to your meditation practice, such as jasmine, rose, or frankincense, to help keep your focus on your surroundings.

Practicing Gratitude

Whether you keep a gratitude journal or spend time sitting in silence expressing gratitude for the good that is in your life, this self-care practice can help you reflect on the things that you are thankful for. Even with an empty nest, there is so much to be grateful for in your life. The fact that your children are grown and they can stand on their own is a good enough reason to be thankful. Waking up each day with the ability to carry out daily activities is more reason to be grateful and optimistic about life.

By practicing gratitude, you acknowledge the good that already exists and shift your focus from your challenges. Gratitude can help you connect with your higher self and increase your happiness. Set aside time each day to reflect on the things you are thankful for. It does not have to be something big, maybe you are grateful for the lady who held the door for you at the coffee shop or for the bouquet of roses your spouse brought you. Write it down in your gratitude journal. Acknowledge the people who are generous and kind to you, thank them for their generosity, and pass the act of kindness to others by being at service to them. It could be in the form of volunteering in your community or at your local church. Volunteering can help you realize how much there is to be grateful for, and it gives you a new perspective on life.

Connecting With a Spiritual Community

If you are religious, attending religious services or prayer group meetings can be a great source of inspiration and can help you connect with your higher self. It also gives you a sense of belonging, strengthens your beliefs, and reinforces your core values. Spiritual groups, such as churches, synagogues, or healing circles, can help you find meaning in life and strengthen your spirituality.

If you are not religious, try a meditation or yoga community and connect with like-minded people. Remember to find a group that aligns with your values for you to receive support and experience healing and empowerment.

Spending Time in Nature

Being out in nature is a great way to disconnect from the busy, everyday life, get in touch with your senses, and find inner peace. Connecting with nature can help improve both your physical and mental well-being. A simple act, such as growing flowers and plants in your garden or being around animals, can help reduce stress, make you feel relaxed, and promote staying active. Being outdoors allows you to feel more connected to nature.

A walk in the woods or going for a hike can help you stay active and inspire your creativity. It can help you stay in the moment and experience your surroundings with all your senses. Besides helping you relax, immersing yourself in nature allows you to be in touch with your spiritual self.

Take a few minutes to reflect on the following:

- *What questions do you seek answers to right now regarding your life?*
- *What spiritual practices are you incorporating into your day, and how are they helping you in your healing process?*
- *What rituals can you incorporate into your daily routine to help you stay grounded?*

Being mindful and intentional about your daily rituals and practices can help you stick to your spiritual self-care routine and tremendously improve your well-being.

Mental Self-Care

The information we feed our minds with greatly influences our mental well-being. Mental self-care involves doing activities that help to clear your mind and reduce stress. Some practices to help you declutter your mind include reading a book, staying away from social media, taking regular walks, and decluttering your house. There is no right or wrong way to clear your mind, what matters is that it leaves you feeling relaxed and improves your psychological well-being. Mental self-care practices include managing stress levels, getting enough rest to rejuvenate your body and mind, staying mentally active by being socially active, and participating in activities that expand your mind, such as doing crossword puzzles, playing chess, or simply joining a book club. Being intentional about maintaining a healthy state of mind can help you develop good habits and practices to help you cope during stressful times.

Prioritizing your psychological health can prevent the risk of mental health issues, such as anxiety and depression. It is important to note that mental self-care does not end with finding ways to help you to relax; it also includes seeking professional help and clinical care if you suffer from severe mental health conditions. To help you improve your mental self-care routine, take time to answer the following questions:

- *What practices help you declutter your mind?*
- *Do you make time for activities that challenge your mind?*
- *What activities do you incorporate into your day that help you stay mentally active?*

Mental self-care differs from person to person. The practices you might prefer to add to your self-care routine will depend on your interests, beliefs, and values. However, the goal is the same and that is to maintain a healthy mind so that you can function at your optimum.

Social Self-Care

Social connections can help improve the quality of our lives. Interacting with others expands our minds and worldview. Engaging in activities that nurture your relationships, such as spending time with friends and family, can help you build strong social bonds and boost your morale. Interacting with others can help you develop good habits for managing stress, which can help you forge your way forward during adverse times. It opens you to different perspectives, ideas, and opinions and helps you see life from a positive viewpoint. Social interactions can also help you cultivate positive mindset skills, such as self-compassion and acceptance. Taking care of your social needs involves making time to catch up with friends and relatives. If you have not interacted with your loved ones in a while, initiating a conversation can feel awkward. Try to be creative in your approach. Perhaps start by sending old photos of your childhood or high school days. It would be fun to see if your friends and family can recognize the people in the photos and reflect on old times.

If you enjoy television shows, consider hosting a movie night or inviting friends over for a game night. With technology making it easy to communicate, you can always jump on FaceTime and connect instantly with friends and family from anywhere. Remember, if someone does not respond to your request to connect, try not to beat yourself up about it. It might not have anything to do with you; perhaps, they are having a bad day. Also, consider people's personalities, not everyone is interested in the same activities. For instance, you could invite a friend for a walk in the park, and they agree because of their love for nature. You could invite the same friend to join a book club, and they decline because they have no interest in it. The goal of social self-care is to nurture your relationships and help you stay connected to the people you love. People's social needs are different. The important thing is to know what your social needs are and create time to do the things you love with the people who matter the most to you.

If you had fallen out with some family members and would like to reconnect with them, start by acknowledging the role you played. Taking responsibility opens a door to rebuilding trust and reestablishing the relationship.

To help you nurture your social life, ask yourself the following questions:

- *How often do you connect with your family and friends?*
- *When was the last time you had dinner together as a family?*
- *What traditions and rituals do you practice to help you nurture your relationships?*

Social self-care is an important dimension in maintaining a healthy life. When we are connected to others, we feel grounded and we thrive.

Professional Self-Care

Practicing self-care in your career and having a self-care routine in place can help you create a work-life balance and increase your productivity. Professional self-care involves doing activities that help prevent burnout and stress that comes with your job. Finding ways to help you manage your psychological and physical health can help you feel relaxed and focused. Having a professional self-care routine in place reminds you that you are human and that will help you feel centered throughout your day.

The following five ways will help you create a professional self-care routine tailor-made for your needs and help you stay focused and perform at your optimum.

Manage Your Time Wisely

Good time management can help you finish tasks in a short space of time. It reduces the stress that comes with the workload and improves your productivity. By following a checklist, you can tick tasks off your list once you complete them and identify which ones you must prioritize. For long-term projects, use a calendar to set deadlines and to time block smaller tasks that are part of the bigger project. This can help you prevent getting overwhelmed. Time blocking your tasks maximizes your productivity and will help you achieve your career goals. By managing your time wisely, you free up time to focus on other areas of your life.

Learning to separate work time from your personal time can help you set boundaries. Communicating your working hours to your colleagues will prevent disputes and improve workflow. There are times you might need to answer a personal phone call at work, as much as there will be times when you have to respond to work emails outside of work hours. Finding ways to avoid distractions, such as limiting personal communications on social media, can help you develop a positive work ethic and manage your time wisely.

Assess Your workload

Keeping track of your projects can help you prioritize important tasks according to their urgency. By prioritizing urgent projects, you limit the time you spend on trivial tasks. Assessing your workload can help you see if you can take on more work or not. While teamwork is about helping your coworkers with their workload, you must know the amount of work you can handle to avoid burnout. If your to-do list is full, be okay with saying no to your coworkers. Knowing how much work you can handle at a specific time will allow you to work in a relaxed manner and help you meet deadlines.

Ask for Feedback

Asking for feedback from your employer and colleagues is not an easy thing to do, but it is an essen-

124 | J.T. HAMM

tial part of your career success. Feedback allows you to assess yourself personally and professionally, but it does not end there. Learning to process, accept, and integrate the information you receive in a way that improves your effectiveness is a skill you have to learn. In asking for feedback, be specific about the area you need feedback on. For example, after a sales meeting, instead of asking *how I do,* you could rephrase your question to *how was my sales pitch and how could I have made it better?* Genuinely asking for feedback can help you learn and improve your skills, identify your strengths and weaknesses, and help you grow professionally.

Take Breaks

Taking a short break during the day to get some fresh air outside can help clear your mind. Doing light stretching exercises in between your breaks will also help you to loosen up and improve your blood flow. Stepping away from your desk for a few minutes can help improve your focus and productivity and help you find creative ways to solve challenges. When you have a difficult task at hand, taking a short break can help you tap into your creative side and find the right solutions. Research shows that taking a break from the task you are working on can help reduce cognitive fixation and enhances your ability to find alternative solutions.

If it has been a while since you last went on a long break, consider taking a few days off to relax and catch up on your errands. If you can afford to be away from work for quite some time, plan a getaway and recharge; you would be amazed at the benefits it will have on your mental and physical health.

Learn to Be Present

Being present in the workplace can help you be intentional about the work you do. When you are fully present, all your senses are alert; you notice the brilliant ideas your not-so-outspoken colleague raised at the meeting, you can hear the acknowledgment from your manager when they compliment your work and you are able to receive praise as well as give it where it is due, and you notice the atmosphere in the office when it changes. Mindfulness makes you aware of your surroundings. Sometimes your mind may wander off to some errand you are supposed to run; however, learning ways to help you stay in the moment can help you perform and communicate effectively in the workplace.

When your mind is calm and you are paying attention, you focus your energy on the things that increase your productivity, such as finishing tasks on time and prioritizing your work and not spending time standing by the water cooler chatting. When you are present, you become a better listener. Focusing on a conversation when a colleague needs your input and being able to provide constructive ideas can help you build trust and dependability among your coworkers. If you have difficulty staying focused, consider taking short breaks during the day to focus on your breathing. Breathing exercises can help bring your focus and attention to your surroundings.

THREE STEPS TO DEVELOPING A SELF-CARE PLAN

An effective self-care plan must align with your lifestyle and personal needs. Having a plan that caters to your needs can help prevent stress, burnout, and getting overwhelmed. Identifying which areas of your life need attention can also help you devise an effective self-care plan. Remember, self-care does not end with creating a plan, putting the plan into action is what will yield positive results. Constantly assessing yourself will also help you track your progress and identify where you are falling short. As you transition, your routine will also change, and your self-care needs might slightly change as well. For example, if you were a full-time parent and would like to jumpstart your career, you might find that your time is limited because of work commitments. You need to create a self-care plan that accommodates your work hours. To do that effectively, consider creating a morning routine and an evening routine for your self-care practices if you cannot make time during the day.

An empty nest is a great opportunity you can use to refocus your attention on your personal needs. Even with a full-time job, you can make time to focus on yourself. It will improve your productivity and boost your mood and help you to be more approachable to your colleagues. The following steps will help you create a self-care plan and decide on the activities you would like to incorporate into your daily routine.

Assess Your Needs

When it comes to creating a self-care routine, there is no one size fits all method of doing it. The first step to creating an effective plan is to assess your personal needs. Your needs and preferences can be a guide in choosing which practices will work for you. Evaluating your daily activities, such as work, and spending time with your family can also help you choose the activities that you can incorporate into your daily routine.

Are you aware of your daily stressors and the things that bring you joy? Awareness of the things that cause you to stress can help you employ strategies to help you cope during a crisis. Being able to identify the things that bring you joy can help you create your self-care plan around them. For instance, you could have a meditation session or go for an evening walk to help you relax and unwind after work. By assessing your needs and evaluating your daily activities, you can create an effective self-care plan that will motivate you to follow through and will not leave you feeling overwhelmed.

Choose Self-Care Activities

After assessing your needs, the next step in creating a self-care routine is to choose activities to incorporate into your daily routine. Identify which activities yield better results for you. For example, if you want to improve your physical wellness, you could set aside time in the morning to listen to a wellness podcast, while working out at home or the gym, and have a healthy, nutritious breakfast before starting your day. If you want to improve your mental wellness, your self-care plan could include listening to a guided meditation and practicing breathing exercises, journaling, and practicing gratitude during your morning and evening routine.

Understanding which areas of your life you need to pay attention to will help you devise a plan that will allow you to bring balance and harmony to that part of your life. For instance, if you have not been spending quality time with your friends and family, you could schedule weekly phone calls or video chats to help you stay connected and nurture your relationships.

Schedule Time to Practice Your Self-Care Rituals

It takes practice to achieve good results in any endeavor. Therefore, self-care will take practice, and it requires constant effort to yield better results. At times, you will succeed in following your plan, and other times you will fall short. The most important thing to remember is to commit yourself to following your plan and accomplishing your goal, which is to create harmony and balance in all dimensions of your wellness.

After choosing the activities that fit into your daily routine, set specific times of the day or days of the week to practice your self-care rituals and stick to them. Following your routine will help you build good habits and prevent you from falling behind. As you progress in practicing self-care, constantly evaluate the activities that work for you and those that are not aligning with your daily activities. Assess the impact your self-care practices are having on your well-being and be okay with removing practices that are not working for you and replacing them with activities that make you feel good about yourself. When you take care of all areas of your life, you increase your efficiency.

An empty nest is an opportunity to focus on your wellness. By making a deliberate effort to take care of every area of your life, you acknowledge your self-worth. Even with an empty nest, you can live a happy and healthy life if you commit to taking care of yourself and creating a balance in all areas of your life.

8

THE SEVENTH STEP TO OVERCOMING ENS

KEEP IN TOUCH WITH YOUR CHILDREN

The early stages of empty nest season can be daunting. You may find yourself fighting the temptation to call your children now and then. While an empty nest is an opportunity for you to focus on yourself and for your child to exercise their independence, staying connected with them can help you heal during the transition. Scheduling weekly phone calls and monthly family dinners, sending them a care package with some of their favorite items, and spending holidays together can help you stay connected. These small windows of opportunity you spend together, whether over a phone call or video chat, allow you to offer your parental guidance and support when it is needed.

It is hard to watch your child grow up even when all you have ever wanted was to see them grow and blossom into responsible adults. After spending years guiding and supporting them, from their diaper days all the way to their teenage years, now they are grown and you have to release them into the world. It is times like these that you wished someone had given you a heads-up on what the end would be like, so you could prepare yourself. Maybe that would have made things easier when you got to this point. Life is unpredictable, but one thing that cannot be taken from you are the beautiful memories you have created from the first day you held your baby in your arms. Every milestone, from their first birthday to the day they called you *Mama* or *Papa,* will forever be ingrained in you. The lessons you have taught and the ones that parenting has taught you are all evidence of how well you have mastered the art of parenting, and now that your nest is empty, it does not mean you are at a loss, it simply means you have done a great job in raising responsible young adults. That alone is worth celebrating. And yes, there may be times you find yourself sitting in your child's room, clutching onto their favorite blanket and thinking about all the fun times you had and the bedtime stories you told each night. Some days you may smile, and other days, you might shed a tear. While reminiscing is a good way to hold onto the beautiful memories of the past, finding ways to connect now is a sure way to create new memories for the future. It is important to schedule times and means of communication that work for both of you and align with your schedules. For instance, you might want to call your child from time to time just to hear their voice, but their schedule may not allow for daily phone calls. Finding a balance in communication will help you both stay connected while maintaining your independence.

PARENTING GROWN CHILDREN

You may be wondering, *Does parenting ever get easier?* Some people may argue that the hardest part about parenting is the early stage of development when a child needs all the love, attention, and affection, and that it gets easier as they grow and can stand on their own. But little is said about what happens when the child grows up. *What happens to the parent-child relationship when the child reaches the young adult stage and their thinking, emotions, and life experiences change?* These elements affect the way both parent and child relate to each other. At this stage of the relationship, the role of a parent changes from primary caregiver to somewhat of a guide or support system. Throughout the transition, there will be differences in views, ideas, and opinions. With all these changes taking place now that your child has moved out, the biggest question you may be asking is *how do I stay connected to my child?*

Let us briefly explore the development of a parent-child relationship. The changes that occur in the relationship happen long before the child reaches adulthood. In the early stages of the parent-child relationship, parenting is about ensuring the toddler is safe, protected, and loved. This stage includes cuddling, dealing with tantrums, and kissing their bruised knees and elbows when they hurt themselves. This is an important stage in a child's development, and the work that a parent puts into ensuring the little being is kept safe should be acknowledged. Eventually, these little beings evolve into adolescence and young adults, and it can be difficult to adjust to the changes. When a child reaches the adolescence stage, their focus is on finding their identity and love and expanding their outlook on life. As the child progresses into their twenties, their identity exploration expands or changes as their experiences, beliefs, and values change. At this stage, the parental role evolves from being the primary caregiver to somewhat of a supportive role. At this point, most parents experience the fear and anxiety that comes with the feeling that their children are making the same mistakes they made. These changes will continue into their thirties and forties as their focus shifts to nurturing grown relationships and their own families.

How do you maintain a strong connection with your grown children? When children move out of the house and gain independence, it can be difficult for them to stay connected with their parents. Even children who love to stay in touch can be limited by distance and finances and may have trouble reaching out often. However, technology has made it easy for us to stay in touch with the world and with loved ones even when we are miles apart. The following strategies will help you form a solid foundation in your communication and help you stay connected with your loved ones.

HOW TO MAINTAIN A STRONG CONNECTION

The ultimate goal of any relationship is to maintain healthy communication where everyone feels safe to share their thoughts, feelings, and concerns. When you build a strong foundation in your communication, you are able to solve conflicts before they escalate to fights and understand each other's point of view. A strong connection with your grown children can help them feel safe to speak to you about the adult challenges they may be facing and allow you to offer your advice and support. However, it is important to know when your advice and support is needed and when it is not needed.

Acknowledge and Respect Boundaries

Setting boundaries is important in nurturing a healthy relationship. Boundaries can help you set limits in your relationships and allow you to express your authenticity. As your children get older, you will notice that the boundaries between you change as well. As a parent, you have always been the one to set the rules around the house; however, as your children mature, they are allowed to put boundaries into place. You may also have your own boundaries that you would like to maintain. Communicate them to your children and help them understand what is okay and what is not okay. When people respect your boundaries, you feel safe and respected; however, when those boundaries are crossed, you feel disrespected and undermined. Identify what boundaries will help you maintain a healthy relationship with your children and recognize what boundaries they have set and respect them.

It is important to remember that when you take in your child's boundaries, you must acknowledge and accept them. At times, they may not make sense to you, and you might not even agree with them; instead of arguing against them, acknowledge that their views and ideas are different from yours, and it is okay. Once you have an understanding of the boundaries between you, it is essential to find effective ways to communicate your concerns. You will not always agree with their world-view, but being an active listener will make your child feel heard.

Recognize Differences

All relationships go through conflicts at some point. As your child grows up, their personality changes and so do their ideas and opinions. As a parent you can choose to accept the difference of opinions and celebrate your child's independent thinking and individual expression. Having different views and lifestyles can bring a different perspective on life and bring you closer to each other.

There will be times when you disagree on the lifestyle choices your children make. Make sure you communi-cate your concerns, make time for conversations, even the hard ones. Setting a foundation for how you handle disagreements can help you find ways to understand their point of view instead of avoiding their unfamiliar ideas. *Imagine a group of friends who call each other regu-larly to catch up on old times and share their values and the exciting details of their everyday lives.* Consider treating your adult children like your friends. Your relationship with them can evolve into an adult interaction if you allow it.

Keep Communication Going

Finding effective ways to communicate with your child will allow you both to make time to communicate in a way that will not leave you feeling overwhelmed. You may be okay with picking up the phone and calling them at any time, but they might not be available for phone calls at the time. Try a different means of communication, perhaps leave a text message or social media comment to let them know you are thinking of them. Finding a medium they love to use can help you make communication easy.

Keep in mind that as your child changes, your role as a parent changes from being completely in charge of their lives to being an adviser. Your advice and counsel will always be needed; however, as valuable as your advice may be, accept that it might not always be implemented. Respond when they reach out to you and listen without judgment or rushing to give advice.

Make Time for Each Other

Maintaining a connection with your grown children requires you both to make the effort. Staying connected and open with each other can deepen your relationship and closeness. As obvious as it may seem, it can be hard to take 10 minutes of your time and call each other as you both navigate your way through separate lives. A simple phone call to say *I love and miss you* can uplift you both.

If you have more than one child, consider creating a group on social media where you all share memories of past times and schedule family video calls. While it can be fun to have your children together and watch them interact with their siblings, whether in person at a get-together or on a video chat, if you want to build a strong connection with them individually, consider making time to spend with each of them alone. Children love their parent's undivided attention, and it allows them to understand their worlds separately as their life experiences change. Staying in touch with your children can help strengthen your bond and make all of you feel valued.

WAYS TO STAY IN TOUCH WITH ADULT CHILDREN

If you have not embraced social media, it is time you consider it. Technology has made it easy to stay in touch with friends and family from all over the world. Distance is no longer a barrier. The following five ways can help you stay connected with the people who matter the most to you.

Connect Through Text Messages and Emails

We all send countless text messages per day, and this is the easiest form of communication that allows you to get hold of a person almost instantly. Text messages and emails allow you to communicate when both of your schedules do not allow phone calls because of work or school commitments. Emailing and texting also allow you to send and receive messages that you can respond to when it is convenient. Text messages are a great way to leave cute messages and reminders of how you love and miss your kids, and it is hard to ignore a text message. Even when they do not respond immediately, chances are, you will hear from them every now and then.

Schedule Weekly Phone Calls and Video Chats

If the traditional means of communication is what you prefer, then plan weekly phone calls when you both have the time and catch up on what is happening in your lives. Ask your child what the best time to call them would be, and plan your weekly calls around a time that is suitable for both of you. Planning ahead will help you manage your expectations and maintain your independence.

Video calling is also another form of communication that allows you to talk to your loved ones while looking at them through the tiny screen of your smartphone. If you both use Apple devices, such as iPhone, MacBook, or ipad, you could use the FaceTime feature for a video calls. Other applications, such as Google Meet, also allow you to talk face-to-face with your children no matter where they are as long as you both have an Internet connection. If you are not tech-savvy, it might be time for you to learn something new. The latest laptop models come with a built-in webcam, all you need to do is download a video chatting software program and connect your webcam to chat with your children. With the high cost of traveling making it close to impossible to stay in touch, utilizing technology can make communication easier. A simple video call can leave you feeling like you were talking to your loved ones in the same room.

Connect on Social Media

Social media platforms, such as Facebook, Instagram, and TikTok, are great means of communication. Though most young adults prefer using Instagram, Facebook is an easy-to-navigate platform that most parents are using. All you need to do is to set up a profile and connect with family and friends by sending them friend requests. With this social media platform, you can send private messages through Facebook Messenger and connect via video chat. You can also view your children's pictures, send videos, and leave comments to let them know you are thinking of them.

If you cannot instantly get hold of them through phone calls, social media platforms allow you to have an idea of what is going on in your child's life when you cannot reach them. However, be mindful not to invade their privacy. Remember, they are experts in their lives even when you do not agree with some of their ideas. Respecting your child's social life and choices can help you avoid tensions and fights and allow them to be open to you while exercising their independence.

For most parents, keeping up with social media can be daunting. If you feel overwhelmed by setting up a profile, ask for help or use other means of communication that will make life easier for you. The goal is to ensure you stay in touch and build a strong connection.

Create Family Traditions and Rituals

Family traditions and rituals bring people closer together. By engaging in activities you share a common interest in, you foster a stronger family bond. Coming together from time to time allows you to engage in face-to-face interactions, share your experiences, and catch up on what has been happening. While technology has made it easy to stay in touch even when you live miles apart, nothing beats the feeling of being in the same room with your loved ones. Most families complain about not spending enough time together because of work commitments. By creating family traditions and rituals, you intentionally make time for each other. It is a great way to change the empty nest atmosphere and feel the warmth and love that comes with having your children close to you. The transition can be hard, but having family rituals can provide you with comfort and help you move forward.

Besides allowing you to maintain a strong connection, family traditions lay a strong foundation for family values you would like your children to carry as they blossom into young adults. If you did not have a family tradition that you practice or you have not taken time to practice your family rituals in a while, it could be time to pick activities that you can do together based on your family values. You could plan a game night and movie night on weekends or get together every holiday season and on special occasions, such as birthday celebrations, to celebrate each other's milestones. Consider having lunch or dinner together on Sundays or plan a yearly family vacation. These activities allow you to spend time together, connect through shared experiences, and help you develop longer-lasting happiness and meaning in your relationship. Family rituals bring everyone together and allow you to do activities that you value as a family and create new memories.

Plan a Monthly Meal They Cannot Miss

While connecting through social media can be rewarding and allows you to stay in touch, no experience can come close to the feeling of sitting together as a family at the dinner table over a family signature dish. If your children live close by, why not plan a monthly get-together? Prepare their favorite meal and have lunch or dinner as a family. It would be an excellent opportunity to hang out in the kitchen while chopping vegetables and preparing the dinner table.

If you enjoy eating out, consider making dinner reservations at your favorite restaurant or setting a day each month to meet over breakfast. You could add a different twist to family dinners and go to a different restaurant each month and try out new cuisines. Consider making this a family ritual you practice monthly, and keep each other updated on what is happening in your lives. Meeting face-to-face can help build a strong connection and bring you closer to your children.

CONCLUSION

Between stimulus and response, there is a space. In that space lies our power to choose our response. In our response lies our growth and freedom.

— (VIKTOR E. FRANK QUOTES (AUTHOR OF MAN'S SEARCH FOR MEANING), 2019)

Now that you have all the strategies on how you can overcome empty nest syndrome, what next? Or perhaps you are thinking, where do I even begin? You might not have the energy to start making social connections and putting yourself in the world again. I can assure you, it is okay. If meeting new people sounds overwhelming to you, why not start your journey by creating a self-care plan? Maybe because you spent most of your adult life taking care of everyone else, you feel guilty about shifting your focus to your needs. Self-care is not selfishness, but it leads to selflessness, compassion, and better relationships. Remember, there is no one size fits all advice for dealing with grief. The goal is to find effective ways that will work for you and help you overcome empty nest syndrome. The journey of parenthood has not ended. This is certainly not the end of the book but the beginning of a new chapter where you get to choose how you want each chapter to look and what you want in it. For some people, being a parent was not something they planned; it was a gift that came unexpectedly and a gift that was welcomed with excitement and jubilation. Welcoming a baby into this world is a blessing, and having the opportunity to be present in their lives from the day they come into this world to when they take their first steps, their first day at school, till the day they graduate from college is more reason to celebrate the journey you have taken to get here.

Difficult as it may be to let go, it is time to welcome the new chapter that is unfolding in your life. Look at it this way, *if you had a blank photo album, what memories would you like to fill it with?* You could create a bucket list of things you look forward to doing that you have always wanted to do and cross them off your list as you accomplish them. If you followed the same routine for twenty-plus years, consider making changes in your daily activities. Do not be afraid to start something new! Whether you would like to go to the gym and work on your physical health goals or you would like to jumpstart your career after years of being a stay-at-home home parent. There is no age limit to starting something new. Learn a new skill, start a business or new career, and polish up your cooking and baking skills by taking a cooking class. The goal is to find activities that you love and focus on what you can do that brings you joy and fulfillment.

Remember, healing can take some time. The pace at which you heal depends on your personality and your social support system. As you transition, you might be reading stories of other empty nesters and searching for answers from different sources to help you gracefully transition. While the internet is filled with advice and tips on how to find healing, be mindful not to compare your journey with other parents. Try not to be hard on yourself when you wake up some days feeling you can conquer the world and other days you find yourself in your child's room crying your eyes out because you miss them dearly. Allow yourself to experience your emotions, and express your feelings even when it is hard to do so. While it is normal to experience grief after children leave home, there is a thin line between symptoms of empty nest syndrome and depression. If you are feeling hopeless and inadequate and grief is taking a toll on your health, consider seeking professional help. Speaking to a competent therapist provides a safe space to open up about your feelings without judgment. Talking about your feelings, the things that make you sad, what you miss the most, and your concerns can help your friends and family understand your viewpoint and can improve communication between you and your loved ones. Being open about how you feel allows the people who love and care for you to experience your authenticity. Remember, prioritizing your mental health and meeting your psychological needs is an essential part of your healing process.

Maybe you are not ready to talk to someone about your feelings, and you need a bit of time to adjust to the transition. Try journaling instead. Consciously, you might not be aware of every thought that lingers on your mind. Writing down your thoughts and feelings can help you identify your thinking patterns. Recording your thoughts in a journal is an excellent practice to help you open up about how you feel without fear of judgment. Journaling can be an exercise for your mind as well. Think of it as a workout for mental wellness, and watch the benefits it will yield to your psychological health and your mood.

Perhaps I have inspired you to jumpstart your career. After twenty-plus years of being the CEO in your home and ensuring that everything runs smoothly and everyone does what is expected of them, you have finally decided that finding a job or starting a business would give you something to look forward to now that the kids have moved out. You might also be considering the possibility of channeling your earnings into your retirement plan and preparing for the future. *Not sure where to start?* Firstly, let me commend you for taking this step. Changing a routine is not the easiest thing to do, but change is necessary to achieve different results. *What are some of your dreams and aspirations that you never got around to accomplishing?* We all have dreams we let die because of limited time and resources. Make a list of some of your dreams, aspirations, and interests, and start building a career around the things you value and have a strong passion for. *Is your house filled with beautiful art paintings from your favorite artists?* Have you always dreamed of painting your own exquisite pieces of art to express your creativity? Why not start a career as an artist by enrolling in an art class? Art is an excellent practice to express your thoughts and feelings through your creativity. If you are a nature lover, you could take a trip to a beautiful, mountainous area with lush green valleys and draw inspiration from mother nature while enjoying the view and the serene sounds of nature. Being outdoors also allows you to engage in physical activities to keep you physically and mentally fit.

This next phase of your life can be filled with beautiful new experiences, valuable lessons, and breathtaking adventures if you choose to take one step at a time and keep moving forward. Look at this season as an opportunity for growth for you and your children, and watch as your lives and relationship blossom. I hope you have found inspiration throughout the pages of this book. I also hope that you will implement the strategies and advice outlined in it and find healing, joy, and meaning in your life. If you found this book insightful, please leave a review on Amazon. I would love to engage with you more and hear your thoughts and feedback.

REFERENCES

AARP Foundation. (n.d.). *8 Ways to create and build social connections.* AARP Foundation Connect to Affect. Retrieved October 23, 2022, from https://connect2affect.org/build-social-connections/

Becca Sangwin, & Beaty, J. (2016, October 28). *How to rescue your marriage from empty nest syndrome.* The Gottman Institute. https://www.gottman.com/blog/rescue-marriage-empty-nest-syndrome/

Brittle, LMHC, Z. (n.d.). *Create shared meaning.* Www.gottman.com. Retrieved October 23, 2022, from https://www.gottman.com/blog/shared-meaning-is-key-to-a-successful-relationship/#:~:text=along%20the%20way.-

Chapman, G. D. (2017). *The 5 love languages: The secrete to love that last.* Christian Art Publishers. https://5lovelanguages.com/

Chavy, N. (2019, January 25). *4 Surprising ways to renew your marriage during empty nest.* LoveWhatsNext. https://www.lovewhatsnext.com/empty-nesters-finding-joy/4-surprising-ways-to-renew-your-marriage-during-empty-nest

Clear, J. (2014, August 27). *The ultimate guide to building a new habit.* HuffPost. https://www.huffpost.com/entry/how-to-build-a-new-habit_b_5699443

Cooks-Campbell, A. (2022, April 22). *9 Tips on how to find yourself.* Www.betterup.com. https://www.betterup.com/blog/how-to-find-yourself

Eatough, E. (2021, August 23). *Seeking help for your mental health is brave. And beneficial.* Www.betterup.com. https://www.betterup.com/blog/seeking-help

Emerson, R. W. (n.d.). *A quote by Ralph Waldo Emerson.* Www.goodreads.com. Retrieved October 23, 2022, from https://www.goodreads.com/quotes/27451-most-of-the-shadows-of-this-life-are-caused-by

Eugene Therapy. (2021, May 13). *Why vulnerability is a strength.* Eugene Therapy. https://eugenetherapy.com/article/why-vulnerability-is-a-strength/

Fidelity Viewpoints. (2022, March 18). *Empty nesters | Tips on downsizing & finances | Fidelity.* Www.fidelity.com. https://www.fidelity.com/life-events/tips-for-empty-nesters

Fluker, C. (2022, May 8). *Why self care is so important.* WhatCherithInks. https://whatcherithinks.com/self-care/

Gibson, A. (2020, October 5). *Hobbies.* The Active Times. https://www.theactivetimes.com/tags/hobbies

Gordon, S. (2020, June 27). *Everything you need to know about the five love languages.* Verywell Mind. https://www.verywellmind.com/can-the-five-love-languages-help-your-relationship-4783538

Gordon, S. (2021, May 30). *How to cope with empty nest syndrome.* Verywell Family. https://www.verywellfamily.com/7-strategies-for-overcoming-empty-nest-syndrome-5180842

Hancock, J. (n.d.). *4 New goals for the empty nester.* JohnHancock. Retrieved October 23, 2022, from https://www.johnhancock.com/ideas-insights/empty-nest-life-goals.html

Hays, K. (2019, March 11). *Five ways to focus on self-care as your empty nest looms.* Grown and Flown. https://grownandflown.com/self-care-empty-nest/

Institute, M. D. (2018, October 1). *Reconnect during the empty nest years.* Marriage Dynamics Institute. https://marriagedynamics.com/marriage-reconnect-empty-nest-years/

Jane. (2021, September 2). *How to thrive with an empty nest: 33 Things to do after the kids leave home.* Jane at Home. https://jane-athome.com/empty-nest-what-to-do/#:~:text=An%20empty%20nest%20provides%20the%20perfect%20opportunity%20to%20explore%20or

John Mordechai Gottman, & Silver, N. (2018). *The seven principles for making marriage work : A practical guide from the international best-selling relationship expert.* Orion Spring.

Kristen. (2019, November 25). *Empty the nest and feel joy again with 19 easy self-care tips.* ACT 2 MOM. https://act2mom.com/empty-nest-feel-joy-again-easy-self-care-tips/

Laura. (2019, September 14). *Empty nest hobbies*. Almost Empty Nest. https://www.almostemptynest.net/empty-nest-hobbies/

LCSW, A. D. (2022, May 19). *How do I stay connected to my adult children?* MyTherapyNYC - Counseling & Wellness. https://mytherapynyc. com/relationship-with-parents-as-adults/

Lind, T. (2018, September 18). *Rebooting goals as empty nesters | The Spokesman-Review*. Www.spokesman.com. https://www.spokesman. com/stories/2018/sep/21/rebooting-goals-as-empty-nesters/

Lisitsa, E. (n.d.). *You are being redirected...* Www.gottman.com. Retrieved October 23, 2022, from https://www.gottman.com/blog/create-shared-meaning-suggestions-from-dr-gottman/

Lisitsa, E. (2012, November 7). *The sound relationship house: Build love maps*. The Gottman Institute. https://www.gottman.com/blog/the-sound-relationship-house-build-love-maps/

Marissa. (2022, May 3). *Family rituals: 100+ Examples, tips, & guide to bring your family closer!* A to Zen Life. https://atozenlife.com/family-rituals/

Morin, A. (2021, April 19). *5 Signs and symptoms of empty nest syndrome*. Verywellfamily. https://www.verywellfamily.com/signs-of-empty-nest-syndrome-4163787

Penny. (2022, October 18). *Parenting grown children: What Dr. Spock forgot to tell us*. Parenting Grown Children: What Dr. Spock Forgot to Tell Us. https://www.grownchildren.net/

Potter, S. (2020, August 12). *Empty nest syndrome: Signs, symptoms, and how to cope*. Choosingtherapy.com. https://www.choosingtherapy. com/empty-nest-syndrome/

Raypol, C. (2022, January 24). *Why should I go to therapy? 8 Signs it's time to see a therapist*. Good Therapy. https://www.goodtherapy.org/blog/why-should-i-go-to-therapy-8-signs-its-time-to-see-a-therapist

S.R, V., & Sachdev, P. (2022, May 22). *Health benefits of hobbies*. WebMD. https://www.webmd.com/balance/health-benefits-of-hobbies

Savage, J. (2019). *Empty Nest, Full Life*. Moody Publishers.

Sergeeva, I. (2021, January 25). *How to stay socially connected to society: Your life depends on it.* Better Up. https://www.betterup.com/blog/how-to-stay-socially-connected-to-society-your-life-depends-on-it

Shultz, M. (2016). *From Mom to Me Again.* Sourcebooks, Inc.

Therapist, M. C., LCSW-NYC. (2016, September 22). *3 Strategies for setting healthy boundaries.* MyTherapyNYC - Counseling & Wellness. https://mytherapynyc.com/setting-healthy-boundaries/

Turner, B. (2011, May 4). *5 Ways to stay in touch with your grown children.* HowStuffWorks. https://lifestyle.howstuffworks.com/family/parenting/parenting-tips/5-ways-to-stay-in-touch-with-grown-children.htm

Viktor E. Frankl Quotes (Author of Man's Search for Meaning). (2019). Goodreads.com. https://www.goodreads.com/author/quotes/2782.Viktor_E_Frankl

Waheeda, A. (2020, June 27). *30 Simple family ritual ideas to bring your family closer.* Messy, yet Lovely. https://messyyetlovely.com/family-ritual-ideas/

Wolfelt, A. (2017). *Healing the Empty Nester's Grieving Heart.* Companion Press.

Wooll, M. (2021, November 17). *The power of human connection: 6 ways to achieve it.* Www.betterup.com. https://www.betterup.com/blog/human-connection

Wooll, M. (2022, January 13). *Empty nest syndrome: How to cope when kids fly the coop.* Betterup.com. https://www.betterup.com/blog/empty-nest-syndrome